The Teacher, the Child, and Music

The Teacher, the Child, and Music

Phyllis Irwin and Joy Nelson

California State University, Fresno

Wadsworth Publishing Company
Belmont, California
A Division of Wadsworth, Inc.

Music Editor: Sheryl Fullerton
Production Editor: Deborah O. McDaniel
Designer: MaryEllen Podgorski
Print Buyer: Barbara Britton
Copy Editor: Yvonne Howell
Illustrators: Susan Breitbard, Joan Carol, Patti Kinley,
Marilyn Krieger, Alan Noyes, Salinda Tyson
Autographer: Melvin Wildberger

Printed in the United States of America

2 3 4 5 6 7 8 9 10—90 89 88 87

ISBN 0-534-05346-7

Library of Congress Cataloging in Publication Data
Irwin, Phyllis A.
     The teacher, the child, and music.
     Bibliography: p.
     Includes index.
     1. School music—Instruction and study.
2. Music—Theory, Elementary.   I. Nelson, Joy.
II. Title.
MT930.17 1986   372.8'7   85-10574
ISBN 0-534-05346-7

To Gladys Tipton

Contents

Indexes

*P*reface

Year after year the authors have searched for an elementary music education text, written specifically for future classroom teachers, that would develop musical skills and understanding regardless of musical background and would enable students to plan and teach music lessons in the classroom. Many writers of texts have attempted to fill this need. However, some present too much information or assume a high level of musical sophistication; others fail to correlate theories and concepts with practical application.

The goal in writing this book has been to present a balanced and practical approach to classroom music for future classroom teachers. This is a book that can be covered in the context of a one-semester or one-quarter course in elementary music education. The conceptual format, which includes activities for teachers and children, encourages and enables future teachers, regardless of musical background, to develop the skills and understanding necessary to plan and direct a classroom music program.

Unique Features

Concept Development

The development of concepts is consistently emphasized throughout the text. Sound, rhythm, melody, harmony, and form are introduced through concepts that parallel those presented in current elementary music series. Hands-on musical activities (singing, listening, playing, moving, creating, and reading) are included as important avenues toward musical under- standing.

Two-Track Approach

The presentation of every concept is followed immediately by a set of activities for teachers and sample activities for children. Future teachers are given many opportunities to reinforce their own understanding of musical concepts and acquire a familiarity with activities suitable for chil- dren. Both teachers and children benefit when concepts are developed in a simple, step-by-step activity-oriented sequence.

Minimum Equipment and Materials Required

The text assumes that many classrooms have limited access to instruments or electronic media. Most of the suggested activities require little equipment and materials. Many can be performed with objects found in the average classroom.

Long-Range Planning Guide

Long-range planning is based on learning theory. Chapter Ten explains how to build a music collection, analyze songs, and plan long-range teach- ing strategies as a basis for concept development. It ties in directly with the concepts and activities presented in other sections of the text.

Mini-Lesson Format

Chapter Eleven shows how to prepare and teach short, well-structured mini-lessons. These mini-lessons, especially designed for classroom teach- ers, are easily presented and integrated into the daily classroom routine.

Emphasis on Singing

Singing is emphasized throughout the book. Suggestions for improving singing skills and step-by-step guides for teaching and leading rote songs enable future teachers rapidly to gain confidence in their ability to teach music effectively.

Song Collection

An extensive song collection includes a large number of children's folk songs and singing games, some of which appear here in print for the first time. Classified indexes direct the teacher to songs that can be accompanied with autoharp or played on melody instruments.

Music Reading

Instrumental and vocal approaches to music reading are outlined in this text. The instrumental approach reflects the influence of Carl Orff in its use of movements, chants, and simple accompaniments. The vocal approach to music reading is based on the Kodály philosophy. Both approaches are presented in a way that can be understood and implemented by teachers without extensive musical backgrounds. An index of songs that are classified by sol–fa and rhythm syllable patterns is included as an adjunct to the suggested reading programs.

Consistent Approach

The approach is simple, direct, and realistic. Verbiage is kept to a minimum and hands-on involvement is stressed. The songs and suggested activities have been tested with adults and children and can be used immediately and successfully in the classroom. The joy of making music is never forgotten. This is the primary consideration underlying *The Teacher, the Child, and Music*.

We gratefully appreciate the suggestions and support given for the original outline and concept by the following people: Edna Hehn, formerly of Sacramento State University; and Ruth Red, Director of Music, Houston Independent School District. Janice Chavez, California State University, Fresno, offered many helpful suggestions regarding the section on children with special needs, for which we are also thankful. The following reviewers were very helpful and offered many useful suggestions: Barbara Bennett, Baylor University; Janice Clark, University of Michigan; Marianne Jacks, University of Houston, Central Campus; Barbara Kaplan, Auburn University; Jeanne Knorr, Towson State University; Sally Monsour, Georgia State University; Mary Anne Norton, Boston University; and Duane Sample, Youngstown State University.

PART ONE

The Program and the Child

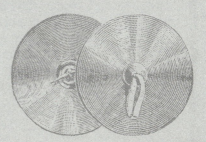

Music plays an important role in the life of a child. Participation in music encourages creativity, promotes individual growth, develops sensitivity and a sense of well-being, and lifts the spirit. As a major form of communication, music is an aesthetic experience, a challenge, and a discipline.

Teachers who consistently incorporate music in the daily classroom routine are well aware of the value of music education. As a future classroom teacher, you will soon have the opportunity to share this precious art form with your students. Your success in this venture will depend, in part, on your knowledge of the abilities of children and the many resources and materials available.

Part One presents an overview of the elementary music program and the background and characteristics of children within the program. Chapter One outlines and defines content and resources: activities, elements, literature, and materials. Chapter Two describes the general behavioral characteristics and abilities of elementary school children, research relative to these characteristics, and the resulting implications for classroom music.

ONE

*T*he Elementary Classroom
Music Program: An Overview

PROGRAM CONTENT

An ideal classroom music program has several general features. First, it involves children in many types of musical activities that allow them to respond to the expressive qualities of music. Second, it provides children with opportunities to develop an understanding of musical structure through exploration of the elements of music. Third, it includes a variety of musical materials. Fourth, it is based on the child's level of development and the ways in which children learn. Each of these aspects of the program is carried out in an atmosphere of positive reinforcement and encouragement.

The assignment of responsibility for classroom music programs varies in different schools. Some school systems hire music specialists who teach music in the elementary classrooms on a regular basis. In other systems, a music consultant, or supervisor, outlines the music curriculum for classroom teachers, teaches classes from time to time, and offers in-service workshops. But often the music program is left entirely to the elementary classroom teachers, who must therefore be familiar with musical activities, elements, literature, and resources including basic series, recorded materials, and classroom instruments.

Musical Activities

Six basic musical activities are appropriate for the elementary school: listening to music, singing, playing musical instruments, moving to music, reading music, and creating music. Children will develop skills in all these activities if given a complete classroom music program.

Musical Elements

A unique set of elements forms the subject matter of music. These elements include sound (sensations perceived through hearing), rhythm (arrangements of sounds and silences in time), melody (the sequential arrangement of musical tones), harmony (the simultaneous presence of two or more pitches), and form (the pattern or design of musical thoughts or ideas in a composition). Under the guidance of the teacher, children can acquire an understanding of these elements as they participate in musical activities.

Musical Literature

In the ideal music program, children perform, study, and listen to music from a variety of sources. They are introduced to traditional songs from their cultural heritage, singing games, part songs, partner songs, and rounds. Eventually they build a repertoire of folk and composed music from both western and nonwestern cultures.

MUSICAL RESOURCES FOR CLASSROOM USE

In the past thirty years, materials designed for classroom music programs have grown in number. School systems can choose from many textbooks, a number of recorded materials, and a fantastic array of classroom instruments. Although the quality of music education depends on you, the teacher in charge, the wealth of available materials will make your job much easier.

Basic Series

Many major American publishers, including Holt, Rinehart & Winston, Macmillan, and Silver Burdett Company, have published music textbooks for use in elementary schools. These series include a colorfully designed book for each grade level, from early childhood through grade eight. Though contents vary, each series contains songs, suggested listening, and instrumental, movement, reading, and creative activities that are appropriate for classroom use. Recordings of the songs and the listening selections accompany all of these major series. Teacher's editions also contain detailed suggestions to help the classroom teacher prepare a year's course of study.

Additional Recorded Materials

As a supplement to the recordings that accompany the basic textbooks, you can build your own record collection from the dozens of albums available in record stores and outlets that specialize in educational materials. This collection can include game songs, music for rhythmic activities, introductions to orchestral instruments, folk songs from around the world, and basic listening libraries. You can also find recordings for use with other areas of the elementary curriculum.

Two excellent series of recorded orchestral music, though not new, are still used in elementary classrooms: *Adventures in Music* (RCA Victor Recording Corporation) and *Bowmar Orchestral Library* (Bowmar Educational Records).* The two series are quite different in format. *Adventures in Music* includes two volumes for each elementary grade level. A detailed teacher's guide accompanies each volume. Suggestions for classroom use are presented along with information about the compositions and their composers. The albums of the *Bowmar Orchestral Library* are arranged by topic. Teaching notes are printed on the inside of each album cover. Large durable charts of selected musical ideas, or themes, from the compositions are also a part of the series.

Classroom Instruments

Each year the collection of musical instruments designed for use in elementary schools becomes more vast and colorful. Such instruments include members of the percussion, wind, and string families. Good classroom instruments enable children to experience a variety of musical sounds as they make music and explore its structure.

Other Sources

School and public libraries offer a wealth of music and music-related material. Song collections, information about music, picture-story books to accompany descriptive music, and stories about composers are on library shelves.

District audiovisual services are also valuable sources of music-related materials. An audiovisual department generally serves as a repository for district-owned film strips, films, and video tapes. In addition, audiovisual services often provide the equipment for showing various media materials.

---

*Lists of the compositions in these libraries are found in the Bibliography.

SUMMARY

The ideal classroom music program involves children in many types of musical activities, provides them with opportunities to develop an understanding of musical structure, and includes a variety of musical materials. It is based on the child's level of development and the ways in which children learn. Responsibility for this program may be left to the elementary classroom teacher.

To implement this program, the classroom teacher must be familiar with musical activities, elements, and literature. Activities include listening, singing, playing, moving, reading, and creating. The elements of music include sound, rhythm, melody, harmony, and form.

The teacher must also be familiar with musical resources. Music series texts, record collections, classroom instruments, and other music-related materials are available for use in the elementary classroom.

SUGGESTED PROJECTS

1. Get acquainted with your school library and look through elementary music textbook series, children's books, and recordings. Begin compiling a list of materials that will be helpful in your classroom.

2. Go to a music store and look at classroom instruments (e.g., recorders, autoharps, and bells). Make a list of instruments, manufacturers, and price ranges.

3. Consult the film and filmstrip catalogs of the audiovisual facilities at your school. Make a list of music-related materials suitable for kindergarten through sixth grade.

*T*he Child in the Classroom

Young children often have had more experiences related to music than to any other part of the curriculum, with the exception of language arts. Left to their own resources, they frequently incorporate music into play. Their absorption in building castles with blocks or sand may be accompanied by quiet humming. The repeated motion of a swing, a bouncing ball, or a jump rope may provide the steady beat for a chant. The counting procedures used in tag games, hide-and-seek, and kick-the-can usually involve rhythmic chants.

Still, the amount of musical experience varies greatly among children of the same age. A few children may live in homes where music is an important aspect of daily life. They play with musical toys, listen to recordings, go to musical events, hear live music in the home, and may take dance or music lessons. Other children may be exposed to music only incidentally, in television and radio shows or religious services. Still others may hear music only rarely. Thus, some children come to school with sophisticated musical skills, whereas others have developed few musical abilities.

In addition to the differences in the development of musical skills among children, there also are great differences in natural abilities. Some children have hearing loss, vision deficiencies, or other limitations that require consideration. Although these varied backgrounds and abilities present challenges for the teacher, all elementary students can learn to enjoy music. Despite their differences, most children share, at each age level, certain behavioral and developmental characteristics.

BEHAVIORAL CHARACTERISTICS OF CHILDREN

Research in childhood growth and development has revealed certain general growth patterns. Though every child is undeniably unique, with individual abilities, behaviors, and needs, the results of this research are still useful, particularly for inexperienced teachers.

Two eminent pioneers in the study of child growth and development are Arnold Gesell (1880–1961) and Jean Piaget (1896–1980). Through careful observation of children, these men identified and categorized general behavioral characteristics and developmental stages. Some of this research has been applied to music education. The following information may be helpful in the *initial* selection of music and activities for various age groups.

Age Five

1. The average attention span is short. Children are frequently restless and need a variety of activity and physical movement. Large overt motions such as marching and walking are appropriate.

2. Interests tend to be limited to the child's immediate experience. Songs are best related to experiences at school and home. Songs about animals and special occasions such as birthdays and holidays are often favorites.

3. Most children can skip, jump, and hop. Their natural interest in dramatic play can be explored.

4. Five-year-olds like to mimic, to mirror, and to copy. Short, repetitive songs that call for physical movement, such as "Eencie Weencie Spider" (p. 230), are enjoyed.

5. Experience must precede intellectualization. Much concrete experience is necessary to give the child a foundation for conceptualization.

6. Many children can focus only on one aspect of a situation at a time. Five-year-olds may be unable to compare phrases or to relate the various musical elements in a song. Though they may be able to step the beat *or* clap the rhythm of a song, they may not be able to do both at once. Though they may be able to clap quarter- and eighth-note patterns, they may not be able to reason that a quarter note and a pair of eighth notes are equal in duration.

Age Six

1. The child continues to learn best through participation: singing, dancing, playing, and moving. Concrete experience is still necessary to conceptualization.

2. Children need to see, hear, and sometimes touch objects to think about them accurately. The effectiveness of a lesson is greatly increased if the central characters or objects described in music are present in the classroom.

3. Six-year-olds enjoy stories with music. This is a good time to introduce orchestral music such as "The Sorcerer's Apprentice" (*Bowmar Orchestral Library*, Volume 59) and "Peter and the Wolf" (Holt, Rinehart & Winston: *Exploring Music*, Grade One).

4. Children love make-believe roles and dramatic play. They like to pretend. They forget they are singing a solo when they become Charlie in the song "Charlie over the Ocean" (p. 162).

5. When comparing equally spaced patterns, children may assume the patterns are the same. If the patterns are unequally spaced, they may no longer seem the same.

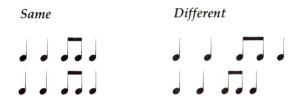

Same　　　　　　　*Different*

The teacher must be careful to write patterns neatly and accurately.

Age Seven

1. Manipulation of objects is still important. Children need to sing, play, move, and manipulate to learn.

2. The realm of magic and magical happenings is of particular interest.

3. Children enjoy working with paper and pencil. The teacher should, however, allow for the long time needed to accomplish written tasks.

4. Seven-year-olds are developing a strong interest in classifying objects and making lists. The teacher might capitalize on this interest by displaying charts of known songs, games, skills, and musical elements.

5. Children may now express strong desires to take private music lessons. They are interested in musical instruments.

Age Eight

1. Children improve in their ability to distinguish between like and unlike melodic and rhythmic phrases. Musical phrases and patterns may be successfully compared and classified.

2. Fine motor coordination is improving noticeably. Words and sentences are better spaced and more uniformly aligned. This may be an optimum time to develop writing skills in music.

3. Children enjoy the use of mystery clues and secret codes. This interest may serve as a motivational factor in the development of reading and writing skills.

4. Many children are now able to intellectualize, after concrete experience, about relationships that involve durations. Children can successfully compare longer and shorter note values and their relationships within the measure and meter.

5. Eight-year-olds are often eager to talk and usually enjoy taking turns. More time can be spent on individual performance, on small group performance for the class, and in singing games and songs that require individual participation.

6. Children enjoy humorous texts. "Don Gato" (see p. 239), a song that describes the adventures of a silly but lovable cat, is a perennial favorite.

7. Eight-year-olds are developing an interest in history and the activities of ancestors. This is a good time to introduce folk songs and dances in conjunction with the study of music from various cultures and historical periods.

Ages Nine and Ten

1. These children enjoy and learn quickly through competition. Rhythm-pattern identification games and mystery-song games can be used with success.

2. The child is increasingly aware of self. Solo-oriented activities may be awkward or embarrassing. Puppets may be an aid to the child who will not sing alone but who can sing through the personality of the puppet.

3. Because children are highly motivated to learn to play instruments, an instrumental approach to making music may be successful.

4. Children are interested in the lives and music of composers.

5. The need for preliminary concrete imagery is diminishing. However, the use of sol–fa syllables, hand signs (see Chapter Twelve), physical movement, and manipulation of objects may still be a necessary part of the child's ability to understand concepts.

6. Ten-year-olds may still have relatively short attention spans. The music lesson should involve several different activities.

7. Children may enjoy taking dictation. This is a good time to emphasize the development of the ability to hear patterns of musical sound and write these patterns in music notation.

Ages Eleven and Twelve

1. This age group is highly competitive. Activities involving individual or team competition are usually exciting and successful.

2. Children want their schoolwork to be related to reality; so the teacher may want to begin by relating classroom music activities to music heard on radio, television, and videos.

3. Many children seem to "love" a subject or "hate" it. Some openly rebel against singing, or against "school music" in general. Teachers may be able to avoid the latter situation by allowing students to choose between two or three different units of study. The creation of special groups, such as chorus, guitar, or recorder, may be a good solution to the problem of varying and increasingly sophisticated needs and interests.

4. Questions such as "What is the largest instrument?" and "Who was the first composer?" are highly motivating. The teacher can easily and successfully investigate these and similar issues in class.

5. Children are increasingly capable of reasoning in the abstract. They are interested in science and mathematics and the "way things work." This is a good time to explore concepts of sound production, investigate electronic music, design and build musical instruments, write compositions, and develop musical scores.

6. Many schools offer a camp program for eleven- and twelve-year-olds. Children are interested in traditional camp songs, and many rich musical experiences, including part singing and folk dancing, can be derived from these seemingly simple songs.

The preceding information will be helpful in planning musical activities for most children. However, some children have special needs. The next section contains information that will help you understand these children and the kinds of musical activities appropriate to their needs.

CHILDREN WITH SPECIAL NEEDS

For many years music therapists and teachers in special education have understood the value of musical activities for students with special needs (those with visual and hearing impairments, physical handicaps, learning disabilities, and mental retardation). Some children who are unable to communicate verbally can express themselves through music, and many children who are unsuccessful in other areas of the curriculum can take pride in their ability to participate in simple singing, moving, or music-playing activities. Music has the power to bring a special kind of light into the lives of the sightless and to comfort and soothe the emotionally disturbed. However, only since the passage of Public Law 94-142 (The Education for All Handicapped Children Act) in 1975 have all classroom teachers had to give consideration to children with special needs. The implications of this act were discussed in the *Music Educators Journal*, Volume 68, No. 8, April 1982:

> The act guaranteed mentally retarded, physically disabled, and emotionally handicapped students appropriate educational experiences. Often this meant bringing these students into the mainstream of music education courses and other regular classrooms. Thus, "mainstreaming" became the catch-phrase for teaching handicapped students alongside normal children. [p. 5]

For those of you who are just becoming acquainted with mainstreaming, the following sections give a brief account of the characteristics of some of the handicapped students you may have in your elementary classroom. Also included are a few activities and materials particularly suited to the needs of these students. Teachers interested in additional information can refer to the bibliography.

Vision-Impaired Students

Children with vision impairment can participate in most musical activities and develop a thorough understanding of the structure of music. Music is one of the arts that does not depend on vision for learning, participation, and enjoyment; thus vision-impaired students can develop aural perception, singing, instrumental, movement, and creative skills. However, these skills will be more easily acquired if lessons emphasize listening, include rote learning of songs and instrumental music, and provide physical assistance in moving to music. Special tactile aids may be effective substitutes for visual aids.

Hearing-Impaired Students

Though children with extreme hearing loss cannot participate fully in as many activities as those with vision impairment, they can take part successfully in some musical activities. Mainstreamed children do not usually have complete hearing loss; most are able to respond in some manner to aural stimuli. Though these children may not be able to learn to sing accurately, they probably can feel the vibrations of a drum or other percussion instrument and respond with physical movement. They can observe and imitate rhythmic motions made by others. With some direction, hearing-impaired children can play percussion instruments with their classmates and play autoharp accompaniments for singing. They can also learn to play melodies on pitched instruments if guided through the notation by a classmate or the teacher.

Physically Handicapped Students

The term *physically handicapped* refers to people who have orthopedic handicaps caused by accidents, birth defects, or conditions such as cerebral palsy. Most physically handicapped students can benefit from participation in music. They can listen, sing, play instruments, and learn to read music. Movement activities, which may pose problems for physically handicapped students, can be adjusted to special needs. Large movements can be replaced by small ones. Rhythmic manipulation of wheelchairs can substitute for locomotor movements. Musical instruments for the class should include some that can be handled easily. Sometimes an extra piece of equipment such as a lap board or special holder can make it possible for the handicapped to use autoharps, melody bells, glockenspiels, triangles, and gongs.

Learning-Disabled Students

The term *learning-disabled* describes students who have learning problems that are not related to innate intellectual capacity. The failure of such children to learn at a normal rate can be the result of organic, genetic, or environmental factors. Some learning-disabled students who are unsuccessful in subjects such as reading, writing, and arithmetic can excel in music. These students should be encouraged to take advantage of this ability and should be given opportunities to develop their potential. With your help, success in music may motivate them to work harder to overcome their deficiencies in other subjects.

Some learning-disabled children find it difficult to master musical skills and concepts. Short lessons presented in a clear step-by-step manner with much repetition will help these students make some progress.

Mentally Retarded Students

Students classified as mentally retarded can develop skills in listening, singing, playing, and moving. The extent to which these skills can be acquired depends on the severity of the handicap. For most retarded children, musical development takes place at a much slower pace than for average children. You can accommodate these children by giving them more time to respond, praising any gains they make, and when possible, helping them make worthwhile contributions to group activities.

Benefits of Music

Mainstreamed students derive many benefits from regular participation in music: (1) successful participation can improve their self-concepts, (2) appropriate interaction with other children during a musical activity strengthens peer relations, (3) participation in musical activities can help anxious or hyperactive children relax, and (4) musical activities can enhance multi-sensory learning (learning involving visual, aural, and tactile perceptions).

Mainstreaming in the Classroom

The first appearance of mainstreamed students in your classroom may make you feel anxious. You may fear that you will be unable to give these students an enjoyable music experience. You may be afraid that you and the other children will be unable to relate to them in a positive way. Such uncertainties are experienced by all conscientious teachers when they face new situations. However, experience with these children and patience and planning with their special needs in mind will enable you and all of your students to have not only a successful experience in music but also a positive experience with the courageous human spirit.

SUMMARY

Children come to school with varied musical experiences and abilities. Some have developed sophisticated musical skills, whereas others have little musical ability. Some children come with limitations that require special consideration.

Research by eminent scholars in the area of childhood growth and development has revealed certain general behavioral characteristics and stages of development. The results of this research are helpful in the initial selection of music and activities for specific age groups.

As a result of Public Law 94-142, many handicapped children are mainstreamed into regular elementary classrooms. Children with visual deficiencies, hearing losses, physical handicaps, learning disabilities, or retardation are among those now participating in many regular school programs. All can benefit from the classroom music program if the teacher takes special needs into account.

SUGGESTED PROJECTS

1. Observe children in informal play and write a description of music-related activities.

2. Select a teacher's edition of a series textbook for a grade level of your choice. Write an evaluation of the activities included with several songs in the text. Discuss the correlation of the activities with the general behavioral characteristics of children at that level.

3. Prepare a brief report comparing the mainstreaming information presented in the teacher's editions of two current music series textbooks (grade of your choice). Discuss the format in which information is presented and the ease with which you feel you could use the teaching suggestions.

PART TWO

Developing Performance Skills

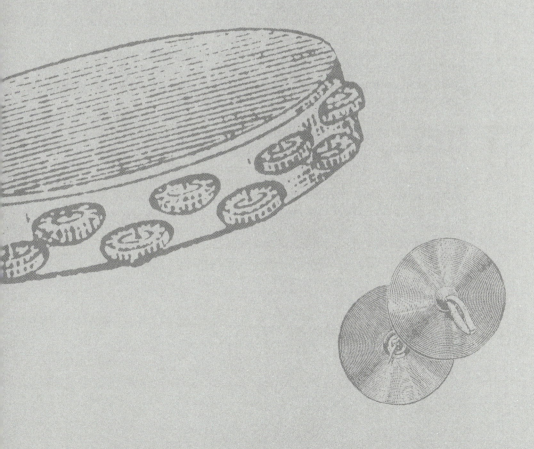

Schools in which music is an integral part of the curriculum have a special feeling that is generated by the joyful participation of children in singing and playing music. This feeling permeates all the daily activities. You will be able to create this special feeling in your classroom if you acquire the necessary expertise. First, you must understand how children develop musical skills. Second, you need to become acquainted with materials and techniques that will help you direct their skill development.

Children learn to sing and play instruments in much the same way that they learn to talk and walk and feed themselves. The skill is modeled for them, they are motivated to perform it, and they have many opportunities for guided exploration and practice.

For the child, learning to sing or play music involves hearing the correct sounds, observing the teaching model (vision-impaired children observe by touching the model as sounds are produced), exploring or imitating the sounds and the physical motions that make the sounds, and practicing the physical motions and sound production.

You, the teacher, can facilitate the skill-development process by providing an atmosphere that motivates children to sing or to play an instrument, a good musical model, many opportunities for exploring vocal and instrumental sound-making, and guided practice.

In the next two chapters you will find materials and strategies designed to help both you and your children enhance your abilities to sing and play music. Chapter Three begins with informal singing for young children and continues with guides for teaching and leading singing at all elementary levels. Chapter Four focuses on playing percussion, strumming, and wind instruments. Your participation in the suggested activities will help you become a better vocal and instrumental performer. As your singing and playing improve, you will gain the confidence necessary for you to become a good model for your children. You will also be able to share the enjoyment that comes from participating actively in musical performances.

THREE

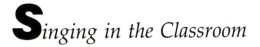

Singing in the Classroom

All children with normal vocal and auditory physiology can learn to sing. With guided practice, most adults whose singing skills were not developed in childhood can also learn to use their voices properly. The techniques suggested on the following pages will enable you and your future students to acquire and improve singing skills. You will also learn methods with which you can teach songs and lead group singing.

SINGING IN THE EARLY GRADES

One of the keys to learning to sing is frequent practice. Daily singing enables children to gain increasing confidence in their ability to sing, provides them with enjoyment, and helps them acquire a repertoire of familiar songs. The following suggestions are useful in planning singing experiences for kindergarten and first-grade classes:

1. Develop a repertoire of short songs with simple melodies for use in the daily classroom routine.

2. Collect short tone-calls you can use with individual children.

3. Identify and work individually with children who have not found their singing voices.

4. Give children opportunities to hear good singing voices.

Singing throughout the Day

Most children's singing will improve without special attention if singing is a part of the daily routine. Songs can be incorporated in opening exercises at the beginning of the school day, and they can be included with other activities throughout the day. Here is a song that can be used as a greeting or as a goodby.

Sing Hello

Nigeria (arr.)

1. Sing hel - lo, sing hel - lo, hel - lo, hel - lo. _____ Sing hel - lo, sing hel - lo,
2. Sing good-by, sing good-by, good-by, good-by. _____ Sing good-by, sing good-by,

hel - lo, hel - lo. _____ Sing hel - lo, sing hel - lo, hel - lo, hel - lo. _____
good - by, good - by. _____ Sing good - by, sing good - by, good - by, good - by. _____

Songs can also set the stage for a change of activity in the classroom. New verses for old songs can be improvised to suit the needs of the unique routine in your own class. Note the verses in the following example.

London Bridge

England

Original: Lon - don Bridge is fall - ing down, fall - ing down, fall - ing down.
1. Now it's time to go out - side, go out - side, go out - side.
2. Now it's time to drink our juice, drink our juice, drink our juice.

Lon - don Bridge is fall - ing down, My fair la - dy.
Now it's time to go out - side, Let's get read - y.
Now it's time to drink our juice, Let's get read - y.

Developing Performance Skills

Some days it is useful to have a song that establishes a peaceful mood for resting. Here is a quiet song for such an occasion. The first verse includes the traditional text; the second verse should be improvised to suit the occasion.

Go to Sleep

France

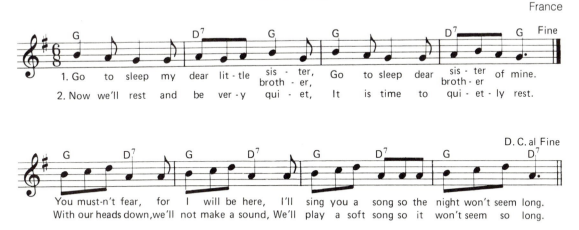

You will find many more such songs in series texts for kindergarten and grade one.

Tone-Calls

Tone-calls also help children improve their singing. Short tone-calls are melodies with two or three pitches. They are used by children throughout the world in playing games, calling each other, and teasing.

The first tone-call can be used for roll call or other occasions when you want to call a child's name.

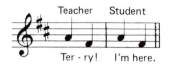

If a student responds on a different pitch, call again, matching the student's pitch.

A variation of Tone-call 1 contains a nice *oo* vowel sound that helps develop a light singing voice. It can also be used to reinforce children's understanding of words, as in the following example:

Variations on Tone-call 2 can be used with the entire class or with individuals. Here is a variation that you can use to make a child feel special.

Teacher to class — Lar-ry has a new shirt.
Class to child — Lar-ry has a new shirt.

Remember, you can change the words, pitches, and rhythm patterns of tone-calls, adjusting them to your class needs.

Children love guessing games. Here is a game for use with Tone-call 1. One child, who is *It*, sits with eyes closed. The teacher quietly touches the head of another child, who then walks up silently behind the child who is *It* and sings:

Child — Yoo hoo, can you guess who?

It answers:

"It" — Yoo hoo, you're _____

If *It* correctly identifies the mystery singer, that child becomes *It* and the game repeats.

Some songs have melodic fragments or motives that can be used as tone-calls. "Old John the Rabbit" is a folk song with a repeated pattern, "Oh yes." The frequent repetition of this pattern enables children to participate immediately in the singing of the song. Students with special needs will be able to join in on "Oh yes" even if they are unable to sing all of the song.

Old John the Rabbit

U.S., collected by John Work

Old John the rab-bit, Oh yes! Old John the rab-bit, Oh yes! Got a

might-y bad hab-it, Oh yes! Of go-ing to my gar-den, Oh yes! And

eat-ing up my peas, Oh yes! And cut-ting down my cab-bage, Oh yes! He

ate to-ma-toes, Oh yes! And sweet po-ta-toes, Oh yes! And if I live,

Oh yes! to see next fall, Oh yes! I won't plant, Oh yes! a gar-den at all.

"New River Train" is a folk song with a good tone-call that can serve as an introduction.

Toot, toot,___ toot! Toot, toot,___ toot!

Developing Performance Skills

New River Train

U.S.

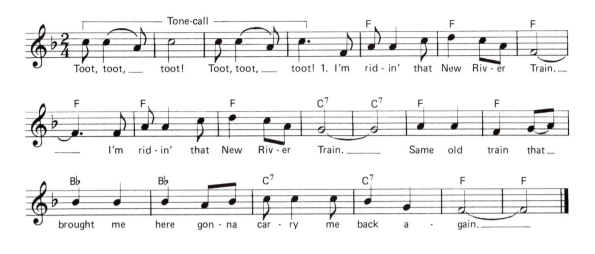

Toot, toot, ___ toot! Toot, toot, ___ toot! 1. I'm rid-in' that New Riv-er Train. ___

___ I'm rid-in' that New Riv-er Train. ___ Same old train that ___

brought me here gon-na car-ry me back a - gain. ___

2. Oh darling, you can't love two, (2 times)
   You can't love two and have it really do.
   Oh darling, you can't love two.
3. Oh darling, you can't love three, etc.
   You can't love three and still love me, etc.
4. Oh darling, you can't love four,
   You can't love four, I won't love you anymore,
5. Oh darling, you can't love five,
   You can't love five and still be alive,
6. Oh darling, you can't love six,
   You can't love six and not be in a fix,

7. Oh darling, you can't love seven,
   You can't love seven and expect to get to
   heaven,
8. Oh darling, you can't love eight,
   You can't love eight, it would be an awful fate,
9. Oh darling, you can't love nine,
   You can't love nine and still be mine,
10. Oh darling, you can't love ten,
   You can't love ten so begin the song again,

You will find other tone-calls suggested in the teacher's editions of series textbooks for kindergarten and first grade.

Working with Individual Children

If your class has been practicing singing every day for several months and some children with normal hearing are still unable to match pitches, individual help is appropriate. These children may not be listening carefully, or they may be confusing singing with speaking. The following activities can help them find their singing voices:

1. Help children to experience the production of higher and lower sounds by

    a. Dramatic use of the voice to portray the different characters in traditional tales such as "Goldilocks and the Three Bears" or "The Three Billygoats Gruff."

    b. Imitation of train whistles or police car sirens.

2. Help children to differentiate between speaking and singing by

    a. Speaking or singing words and short phrases and then asking a child to classify each example as singing or speaking.

    b. Inviting a child to first speak and then sing the first word of one of the tone-calls presented on page 22. Starting on the child's pitch, sing the entire tone-call. Then ask the child to sing it.

Even though you may not notice much progress the first time you give individual assistance to a child, don't despair. Be encouraging and praise the slightest improvement, remembering that all people with normal hearing and vocal mechanisms can learn to sing. With some, the process simply takes longer.

HELPING OLDER CHILDREN IMPROVE THEIR SINGING

By the end of third grade, most children should be singing in tune (singing songs with accurate pitch). The following paragraphs describe ways to help those who still have difficulty.

Listening Skills

Many children who sing out of tune have never developed good listening skills. These children will be able to sing with greater accuracy when they learn to differentiate aurally between higher and lower pitches and to perceive melodic contour. Activities described in Chapter Seven may be used to improve listening skills.

Short Vocal Exercises

Short vocal exercises are helpful in the development of singing skills. Excerpts from songs the class is singing may be used to help children extend their vocal ranges (see p. 32). These short passages can be sung at a slower tempo. Here are some songs you could introduce in grades four through six. Useful excerpts are marked in brackets.

Hop Up! My Ladies

U.S.

Did you ev-er go to meet-ing, Un-cle Joe? Un-cle Joe? Did you

ev-er go to meet-ing, Un-cle Joe?__ Did you ev-er go to meet-ing, Un-cle

Joe, Un-cle Joe? Don't mind the weath-er, so the wind don't blow.

Hop up, my la-dies, three in a row, Hop up, my la-dies, three in a row.

Hop up, my la-dies, three in a row, Don't mind the weath-er, so the wind don't blow.

The Cuckoo

Austria

1. O I went to Pe-ter's flow-ing spring Where the wa-ter's so good, And I
2. Af-ter Eas-ter come sun-ny days That will melt all the snow; Then I'll
3. When I've mar-ried my maid-en fair, What then can I de-sire? O a

heard there the cuck-oo As she called from the wood.
mar-ry my maid-en fair, We'll be hap-py, I know.
home for her tend-ing And some wood for the fire.

REFRAIN

Ho - li - ah, Ho - le-rah - hi - hi - ah, Ho - le-rah cuck-oo! Ho - le-rah - hi - hi - ah,

Ho - le-rah cuck-oo! Ho - le-rah-hi-hi-ah, Ho - le-rah cuck-oo! Ho - le-rah-hi-hi-ah - ho!

The Keeper

England

A keep-er would a - hunt-ing go, And un-der his cloak he car-ried a bow,

All for to shoot at a mer-rie lit-tle doe, A-mong the leaves so__ green, O!

To help improve diction, tone production, and singing range, children can practice short exercises such as the following:

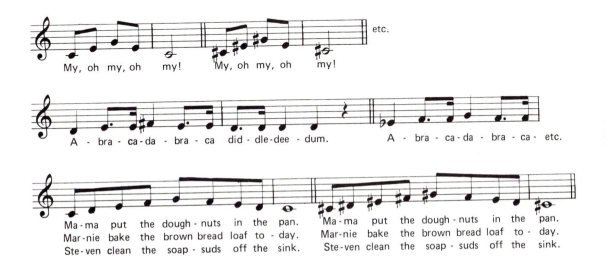

Sing each exercise several times, moving up by half steps. Because these exercises help develop an ability to keep the breath flowing smoothly, they may be helpful for children who stutter. If modeled slowly in close proximity, they can also improve the diction of some children with limited hearing.

Instrumental Reinforcement

Pitched instruments such as bells or xylophones can sometimes help children improve their ability to sing in tune. Experimenting with a set of bells—playing notes and then trying to match them vocally—can improve the coordination between ear and vocal intonation. Once children can match a few pitches, they can sing simple chants and use these chants as accompaniments for familiar songs. Reinforced by a group of confident singers, and bells or other pitched instruments, uncertain singers should begin to feel more secure.

Here are two songs with simple chants that can be played and sung by less certain singers. "Down by the Station" can be used in grades two or three. "Sourwood Mountain" is appropriate for grades four, five, or six. "Down by the Station" is preceded by a short chant that can be sung repeatedly as an accompaniment.

Down by the Station

U.S.

The chant for "Sourwood Mountain" is written as a second part through the entire song.

Sourwood Mountain

U.S.
Arranged by Phyllis Irwin

Models for Children

All children will find it easier to sing well and in tune if they frequently hear models of correct singing. Though it is not necessary to have a highly trained voice to be a good model for children, you should seek to improve your own singing and become familiar with other models.

If a song is sung correctly the first time it is presented, children will master it much more easily and quickly. Practice each new song carefully before introducing it to your class. You may want to use a recording to help yourself learn the song.

Recordings can also be used as models for classroom singing. All of the songs in the current elementary music series are recorded, some with adult voices and many with children's voices. These recordings are ideal models for students. With a phonograph in your room and a recording in hand, you can feel confident that your children will hear new songs sung correctly.

SELECTING SUITABLE SONG MATERIALS

Most public schools provide state-adopted series textbooks that are organized by grade levels. These series are prime sources of suitable songs. Songs in series textbooks have been selected and arranged so that you can be certain that the range, text, and style will suit your grade level.

You can build a file of additional songs by looking through folk song collections, children's song books, and recreational song collections. These sources are available in public libraries, public school curriculum centers, central school libraries, and libraries in colleges and universities.

As a classroom teacher, you will be interested in finding songs that enhance other areas of the curriculum, such as social studies, language arts, and mathematics. You may want to collect special songs for Halloween, Thanksgiving, Channukah, Christmas, and Valentine's Day, songs for fun, songs for quiet times, and action songs. Criteria for selecting songs should include:

1. Appropriate range.

2. Appropriate length: relatively short for young children.

3. Appropriate level of difficulty. A series textbook can be used as a guide.

4. Appropriate text. Consider the age and interests of children (see pp. 8–11).

There should also be agreement between the rhythm of the music and the natural rhythm of the words and syllables in the text; that is, stressed words and syllables should fall on stressed or accented beats.

LEADING GROUP SINGING

One facet of your role as music educator is that of song leader. As song leader you must be able to sound a starting pitch, establish a tempo, and indicate exactly when the group should begin to sing. Therefore, you need to practice the techniques in this section until you feel comfortable in the role of song leader. (For more specific conducting gestures, see Chapter Six.)

Two Methods for Starting Songs

Many educators believe that the best technique for starting a song is to begin by singing or playing serially the first, third, and fifth notes of the scale, the **tonic chord,** to establish a sense of the tonality of the song (see p. 193). To use this technique you must become familiar with the sound of the tonic chord in both major and minor.

Major tonic chords sound like this:

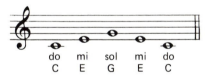

Minor tonic chords sound like this:

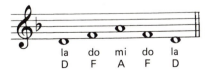

Here are tonic chords for a few keys frequently found in series textbooks and song collections. Practice singing these chords until you can sing them accurately and easily.

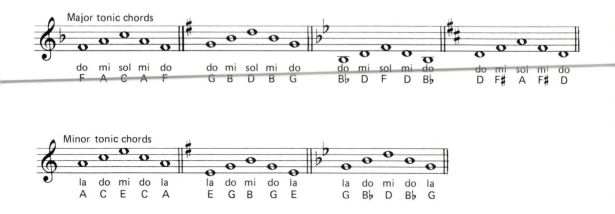

Once the tonic chord of a song is established, sound the starting pitch and establish the tempo by chanting a few beats on the starting pitch. Cue the class to start by chanting a word such as *sing* or *begin*.

Another technique for starting songs suggests that you sound the starting pitch of the song, establish the tempo, and cue the beginning as above. This method is simpler than the tonic-chord approach but does not establish a feeling of the tonality of the song.

Regardless of the approach used, it is necessary to have an instrument that can produce the starting pitch. Chromatic pitch pipes (available at most music stores), melody bells, keyboard instruments, or autoharps can be used.

Songs to Sing and Lead

Here are some songs with guidelines for starting them.

Somebody's Knocking

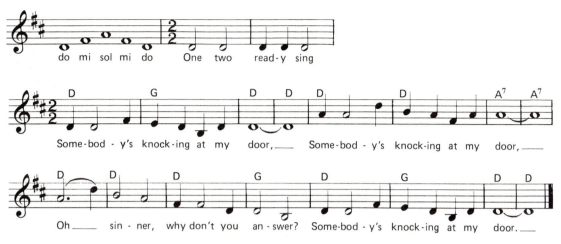

do mi sol mi do One two read-y sing

Some-bod-y's knock-ing at my door,___ Some-bod-y's knock-ing at my door,___

Oh ___ sin-ner, why don't you an-swer? Some-bod-y's knock-ing at my door. ___

Michael Row

do mi sol mi do. One read-y sing:

Mi-chael row the boat a-shore, Hal-le-lu-

jah. Mi-chael row the boat a-shore, Hal-le-lu-jah.

Music Alone Shall Live

Germany

do mi sol mi do   One two three   one read-y sing:

1. All things shall pass a-way, both earth and sky, Mu-sic a-lone shall live,

Mu-sic a-lone shall live, Mu-sic a-lone shall live, it shall not die.

Drunken Sailor

Sea Chantey

la do mi do la   One two   read-y sing

Verse

1. What shall we do with a drunk-en sail-or, What shall we do with a drunk-en sail-or,

What shall we do with a drunk-en sail-or, Ear-ly in the morn-ing?

Refrain

Hoo - ray and up she ris - es, Hoo - ray and up she ris - es,

Hoo - ray and up she ris - es, Ear - ly in the morn - ing.

Optional descant

Hoo-ray, Hoo-ray, Hoo-ray, Hoo-ray. Hoo-ray, Hoo-ray, Ear-ly in the morn-ing.

2. Put him in the brig until he's sober,
   Put him in the brig until he's sober,

Put him in the brig until he's sober,
Early in the morning.

Practice these songs. Form a small group with a few of your classmates and take turns starting the songs. Once you feel secure as a song leader, you will be ready to develop a set of procedures for teaching songs.

TEACHING A SONG BY ROTE

Short repetitive songs can be taught by **rote** (through imitation). Rote teaching is necessary for children who do not know how to read music. Two methods of rote teaching—*whole song* and *phrase-by-phrase*—are in common use. The whole-song method offers children many opportunities to hear a song correctly performed. Techniques include a discussion of the text, the use of appropriate motions, and an invitation to join in on short repeated **phrases**. Any techniques that promote children's attention to what they hear (*aural attending*) are helpful to children who are vision-impaired, learning-disabled, or mentally retarded.

"The Whistle of the Train" is an example of the kind of song that can be taught by the whole-song approach. It is short, the words are simple, and the melody contains repetition. Suggestions for presenting this folk song (appropriate for kindergarten through grade two) follow the music.

The Whistle of the Train

Congo

Pio, pio, pio, ____ Pio, pio, pio, ____ The whis-tle of the train is go-ing Pio, pio, pio. It's com-ing round the bend and blow-ing Pio, pio, pio.

From *UNICEF Book of Children's Songs*, edited by William I. Kaufman. Stackpole Books, 1970. Reprinted by permission.

Teaching Procedure

1. Present motivation (a picture, poem, or question to elicit student response).
2. Ask the children to listen for the short word that imitates the whistle sound.
3. Sing the song for the children.
4. Discuss the word *Pio* (pronounced as one syllable, *pyo*).
5. Ask the children what the train is doing.
6. Sing the song again and invite the children to rub their hands together to imitate the sound of the train as they listen to the song once more.

7. Sing the song a third time, inviting the children to sing along with their inside voices (to sing only in their imaginations).

8. All sing the song together.

9. If children have difficulty with the words, go over the problem spots, chanting the words rhythmically and asking them to echo you.

The phrase-by-phrase approach to teaching a song by rote divides a song into smaller sections or phrases (see p. 135). Once children have heard the whole song, the teacher sings or plays a phrase and invites the children to imitate. One by one, all parts of the song are modeled and imitated until the children can sing the entire song accurately.

The American sea chantey "Fire Down Below" is a song that can be taught effectively by the phrase-by-phrase method. Teaching suggestions follow the music.

Fire Down Below

Teaching Procedure

1. Present motivation (a picture, poem, or question).

2. Invite the class to listen carefully for answers to the following questions as you sing the song for them:
   a. Where is the fire?
   b. Did the cook know about the fire?
   c. Who is going to bring a bucket of water?

3. Sing the song.

4. Discuss answers to the questions.

5. Using a my-turn–your-turn technique, sing the song phrase by phrase:

Teacher:	There's a fire up aloft, There's a fire down below,
Children:	There's a fire up aloft, There's a fire down below,
Teacher:	Fire in the galley, But the cook didn't know.
Children:	Fire in the galley, But the cook didn't know.
	etc.

6. Review any problem phrases.

7. Sing phrases in groups of two and invite the children to echo.

8. Sing the song for the children once more, suggesting that they sing along with their inside voices.

9. Invite the children to sing the song through by themselves. Support can be provided by an accompanying instrument such as the autoharp.

The whole-song and phrase-by-phrase techniques will help you teach songs by rote. In the next section you will find methods for teaching part singing.

TEACHING PART SINGING

Once children can sing accurately in unison, they can participate in **part singing** (singing in harmony). Part singing, if it is done well, can be one of the most satisfying performances in an elementary classroom. Children enjoy and take pride in being able to sing harmony. It is important, therefore, to understand how you can help your students develop part-singing skills.

Children can participate in several kinds of part singing. The progression, in terms of difficulty, usually follows this sequence: adding a chant to a melody that has been previously learned, singing rounds and partner songs, adding descants to melodies, and singing parallel harmonies. Each of these forms of part singing is defined and discussed in the following paragraphs.

The easiest form of part singing, usually introduced in second-grade books, combines a familiar melody with a simple chant. The following is an example of a song that can be sung with a **chant** (a short melody sung over and over again).

Bought Me a Dog

U.S.

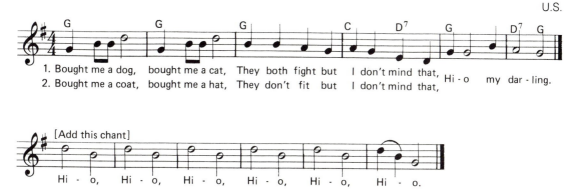

1. Bought me a dog, bought me a cat, They both fight but I don't mind that, Hi - o my dar - ling.
2. Bought me a coat, bought me a hat, They don't fit but I don't mind that,

[Add this chant]

Hi - o, Hi - o, Hi - o, Hi - o, Hi - o, Hi - o.

Suggested Teaching Procedure

1. Teach the song as a unison song.

2. When the children can sing it independently, add the chant with your own voice or a melody instrument.

3. Invite a small group of children to sing the chant with you or with the instrument.

4. After the children have had several opportunities to practice the chant, let them try it independently. If the children falter, add vocal or instrumental support.

Another form of part singing is the traditional **round**, an imitative song in which one group begins singing the melody and, upon reaching a certain point, is joined by another group singing the melody from the beginning. Some rounds involve four different groups. Here are four rounds, one for children in grades two and three, the others with appeal for older students.

The Alphabet

Traditional

A b c d e f g, H i j k l m n o p, Q r s t u v, Dou-ble u and x y z, Now I know my A B Cs, Next time won't you sing with me.

Ghost of Tom

Have you seen the ghost of Tom, Long white bones with the flesh all gone?____

Oh, _____ Would-n't it be chil-ly with no skin on?

Toembai

Israel

Toem-bai, toem-bai, toem-bai, toem-bai, toem-bai, toem-bai, toem-bai. Aye-da-da, da-da-da-da-da, aye-da-da-da-da. Aye-da-da-da-da, aye-da-da-da-da, aye-da-da-da-da-da.

By the Waters of Babylon

Philip Hayes

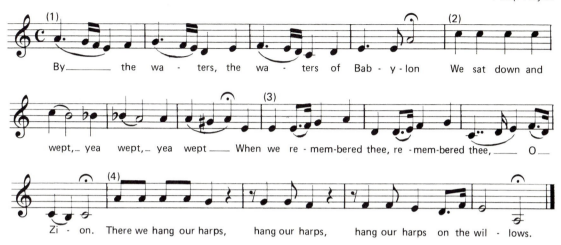

By ___ the wa - ters, the wa - ters of Bab - y - lon We sat down and wept, _ yea wept, _ yea wept ___ When we re - mem-bered thee, re - mem-bered thee, ___ O _ Zi - on. There we hang our harps, hang our harps, hang our harps on the wil - lows.

Teaching Procedure

1. Teach first as a unison song.

2. When the children can sing it independently, add a second part with your voice or an instrument.

3. Divide the class into two balanced parts and try the song as a two-part round.

4. When and if your class is ready, add additional parts.

"Music Alone Shall Live" (p. 36), "Shalom Chaverim" (p. 63), "Little Tom Tinker" (p. 61), "Rose, Rose" (p. 153), "Hey Ho, Nobody Home" (p. 247), and "Canoe Song" (p. 123) are other songs in this text that can be sung as rounds.

Some songs can be sung simultaneously to create a satisfying harmonic effect. Songs combined in this way are called **partner songs**. "Swing Low, Sweet Chariot" (p. 243) and "All Night, All Day" (p. 244) can be sung as partner songs.

Many songs can be accompanied by **descants** (independent melodies that accompany primary melodies). Songs with descants usually appear in series textbooks in grade three. The procedures for teaching songs with descants are basically the same as those for teaching songs with chants. Here is a song with an easy descant.

This Train

U.S.
Arranged by Phyllis Irwin

Older students will enjoy singing the following song with a descant.

The Water Is Wide

England
Arranged by Phyllis Irwin

Many people enjoy harmonizing "by ear" while sitting around a campfire at night or when traveling in a car. Harmonizing in this manner often involves adding a second part that moves parallel to the melody. Series texts may introduce two-part parallel harmonizing as early as grade three. Books for grades four, five, and six include songs in which a second part moves in parallel thirds or sixths with the melody. Preparatory activities for singing these songs include (1) listening to parallel thirds or sixths played on pitched instruments, (2) guided listening to recordings of appropriate songs from the basic series texts, and (3) singing the melody while an instrument plays a parallel harmony part.

Here is a song with a short two-part section with parallel thirds.

I'm Gonna Sing

U.S.

I'm gon-na sing when the spir-it says sing;___ I'm gon-na sing when the spir-it says

sing;___ I'm gon-na sing when the spir-it says sing, and o-bey the spir-it of the Lord.___

Some part songs incorporate more than one style of harmony.

Ezekiel Saw a Wheel

U.S.
Arranged by Phyllis Irwin

Practice your part-singing skills as often as possible. Harmonizing is one of the musical activities that both you and your children will enjoy.

SUMMARY

All children with normal vocal and auditory physiology can learn to sing. As a teacher, you must be familiar with techniques that enable children to develop singing skills. Activities that will help younger children find their singing voices and improve singing skills include:

1. using songs in the daily routine
2. using tone-calls with individual children
3. providing good singing models
4. working individually with children who are having problems
5. helping children experience the production of higher and lower sounds
6. helping children differentiate between singing and speaking

After third grade, most children should be singing songs on pitch. If these older children still experience singing difficulties, you can help by

1. emphasizing listening skills
2. practicing short vocal exercises
3. reinforcing voices with pitched instruments

Suitable songs are available in state-adopted textbooks, folk song collections, children's song books, and recreational song collections. It is helpful to make a collection of songs that will be appropriate for use with other subjects and for special days.

Two musical elements must be established to have a group of singers begin a song at the same time: the pitch of the first note and the tempo, or rate of speed, of the song. One method for starting a song includes preparatory singing of the tonic chord, sounding the starting pitch, and establishing the tempo. A second method involves sounding the first pitch of the song and then establishing the tempo.

Short repetitive songs can be taught by rote. There are two basic rote song-teaching methods: the whole-song method and the phrase-by-phrase method.

Part singing can be taught as early as second grade. Types of part songs suitable for elementary school children include melodies accompanied by chants, rounds, partner songs, songs with descants, and songs with parallel harmony.

SUGGESTED PROJECTS

1. Collect a repertoire of ten songs appropriate for the grade of your choice. Learn to sing these songs accurately and be able to start them with the procedures suggested in this chapter.

2. Get acquainted with teacher's editions and song recordings from three current music series textbooks, grade of your choice. Compare teaching aids, quality and special features of the recordings, and choice of songs.

FOUR

Playing Instruments in the Classroom

Musical instruments add a colorful dimension to classroom music. They can provide accompaniments for songs, help teach musical concepts, and be used for improvisation.

There are three categories of classroom instruments: percussion, strumming, and wind. Percussion instruments include drums, shakers, scrapers, wooden hitters, ringers, and pitched bells or bars. Strumming instruments include autoharps, ukuleles, and guitars. The wind family includes tonettes, flutophones, and recorders. This chapter explores techniques and procedures for playing and using commercial and handmade percussion instruments, autoharps, ukuleles, guitars, and the soprano recorder.*

PLAYING PERCUSSION INSTRUMENTS

The following list of useful classroom instruments belonging to the **percussion family** includes suggestions for effective substitutes and commercially available instruments.

---

*The soprano recorder has the widest range of all recorders and produces the best sound.

Type	Commercial	Easily Made Substitutes
Drums	Hand drum; tom tom; conga; bongo	Coffee can with plastic lid or nail keg with tightly stretched inner tube over end
Shakers	Tambourine; maracas	Aluminum or plastic container filled with rice, beans, or BBs
Scrapers	Sand blocks	Small wood blocks covered on three sides with sandpaper
	Guiro (wee-ro); reco reco (ray-co ray-co)	Dried gourd with notches filed across it and nail for scraping
Wooden hitters	Clavés; rhythm sticks	Hardwood dowels; broom handles cut into 6-inch lengths
Ringers	Triangles; finger cymbals	Steel nails or bolts suspended by fine wire or fishing line, with nails for strikers
	Jingle bells	Jingle bells sewed on elastic bands for small wrists or ankles
	Gongs	Large oil drum lid suspended with heavy strap, with a beater made of $\frac{1}{4}$-inch dowel inserted into a $1\frac{1}{2}$-inch rubber ball wound with yarn
Pitched bells	Melody bells; resonator bells; step bells; hand bells	Tuned water glasses

Schools often have a collection of percussion instruments. While specific uses for these instruments are described in Parts Three and Five of this book, some general background information and suggestions can help you plan and direct percussion activities.

Procedures

Because children are highly enthusiastic about percussion instruments, your first task is to set up orderly procedures for hands-on experiences. These procedures should include:

1. special routines for setting up the instruments and putting them away
2. establishment of clear signals for starting and stopping together
3. a plan that will enable all children to have instrumental experiences

Instrumental activities will flow more smoothly if you have help with logistics. Classroom monitors can assist by getting instruments out and putting them away carefully at the end of each lesson. It may be helpful

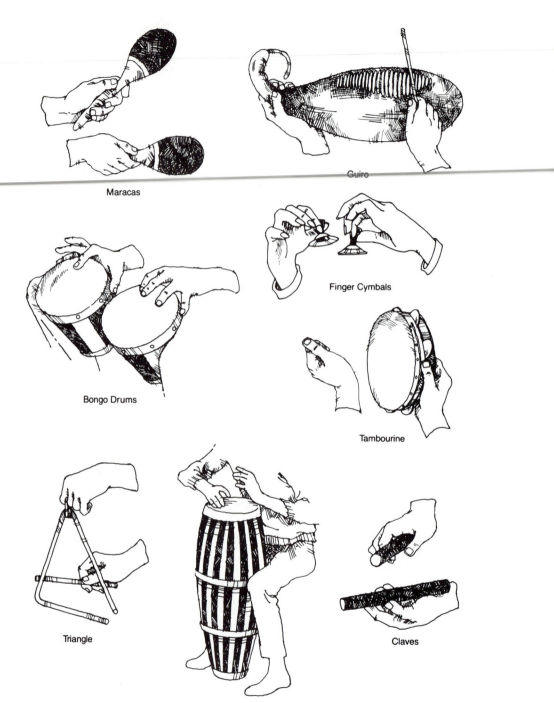

Maracas

Guiro

Bongo Drums

Finger Cymbals

Tambourine

Triangle

Conga Drum

Claves

to place instruments in front of children—on their desks or on the floor—rather than in their hands.

Signals for starting together can be similar to those for classroom singing. Visual cues or hand signals can be used to indicate when the group should stop playing. Be sure to use these signals during the first lesson and have children practice starting and stopping together.

Selection of children to participate in instrumental activities depends on the nature of the lesson. If the lesson is exploratory, each child should have an opportunity to play. If the goal of the lesson is to perform an instrumental accompaniment to a song or to play from notation, you may want to be selective. Give the entire class an opportunity to practice the rhythm of each part, then give the instruments to those who are able to perform accurately. Keep a record of those who play so that you can give others the opportunity in future lessons.

To obtain the best sound, percussion instruments should be held in a way that permits them to vibrate freely. Most hand drums have a lower opening that has to be left open for good sound production. Triangles are held lightly by the suspension loop and tapped quickly. Sticks and claves must also be held lightly so the wood can vibrate.

Percussion Instruments and Mainstreamed Students

Many orthopedically handicapped children and those with hearing disabilities can play nonpitched percussion instruments. Children with minimal mobility of one hand or arm can use a striker or mallet to tap triangles, small drums, or other light percussion instruments suspended from a frame. If the arm is mobile but the hand unable to grasp, the striker or mallet can be fastened to the mobile arm with an elastic strap. Hearing-impaired children can suspend small nonpitched instruments close to an ear and strike them as the teacher signals rhythmically. In this way they can produce and hear sounds as part of the group activity.

Techniques for Mallet Instruments

Some schools have pitched percussion instruments designed for children by the German composer Carl Orff (see Chapter Thirteen). These instruments include glockenspiels, xylophones, metallophones, and small timpani. With the exception of the timpani, the instruments have metal or wooden bars that are played with mallets. If you are able to obtain Orff-type instruments for your classroom, you will need to learn and be able to teach correct mallet technique.

Initially, mallet technique grows out of children's body movements.

As preparation for playing a **bordun*** accompaniment, children can pat their thighs to a steady beat. If mallets are to be played alternately, pat the thighs (**patsching†**) with alternate hands. An important point to keep in mind is that you serve as a model for your children. Face your class and perform the desired movement in reverse. (Remember, if you want children to start with their left hand, you must start with your right hand, and vice versa.)

When the patsching is transferred to the instruments, one should concentrate on holding the mallets as if holding the handlebars of a bicycle. Keep the elbows up, away from the sides of the body, and strike the bars lightly but firmly. After striking, allow the mallets to bounce up quickly from the bars. (Holding the mallets on the bar stops the sound.)

Here are some patterns that can be played on mallet instruments. In these exercises, the notes with the stems coming down are for the left hand. The notes with the stems going up are for the right hand. "Row, Row, Row Your Boat," "Three Blind Mice," and "Hot Cross Buns" can be accompanied by any one or any combination of these four patterns.

Preparation   Children patsch with both hands, performing the notated rhythm.

Preparation   Children patsch with both hands, performing the notated rhythm.

---

*A bordun is an accompaniment pattern in which two pitches, played simultaneously, are repeated over and over.

†*Patsching* and *patsch* are derived from the German word *patschen*. These words are used to refer to patting or slapping the lap or the tops of the thighs.

Preparation   Children pat left hand on top of left thigh, then right hand on top of right thigh.

Preparation   Children pat left, pat right, cross left hand over to pat outside of right thigh, and then pat with right hand again.

Here are a bordun and two ostinati that can be played on mallet instruments to accompany "Chatter with the Angels" (next page) and "Turn Your Glasses Over" (p. 211). (An **ostinato** is a short melodic pattern sounded over and over again.)

Preparation   Patsch with two hands, following rhythm of the bordun.

Preparation   Patsch first with left hand and then right hand, following rhythm of the ostinato.

Preparation   Pat top of right thigh with right hand, top of left thigh with left hand, cross right hand over to pat inside of left thigh, then pat top of left thigh with left hand.

Chatter with the Angels

Spiritual

Chat - ter with the an - gels ear - ly in the morn - ing, chat - ter with the an - gels

in that land. Chat - ter with the an - gels ear - ly in the morn - ing,

chat - ter with the an - gels, join that band! I want to join that band and

chat - ter with the an - gels all day long! I want to

join that band and chat - ter with the an - gels all day long!

Developing Performance Skills

PLAYING STRUMMING INSTRUMENTS

The autoharp, the simplest strumming instrument to play, adds color to classroom music. Four- and five-year-old children are thrilled when given an opportunity to strum the autoharp while you press the buttons. Six- and seven-year-olds can double up to play accompaniments, one pressing the buttons and the other strumming. Older children can play the instrument by themselves.

Twelve-bar autoharps, available in many schools, can be used to accompany many of the songs in this book and in music series textbooks (chord names are printed above the melody line). Children can practice, one or two at a time in a music corner, strumming lightly with a soft felt pick, rubber eraser, or thumb.

Orthopedically handicapped children can usually find a way to strum while someone else presses the buttons. Hearing-impaired children can also use strumming instruments, pressing the buttons and strumming. Vision-impaired children can strum, with other children pressing the proper chord buttons (or showing them how).

On the next page is a diagram of the arrangement of chord buttons on the typical 12-bar autoharp. The buttons are arranged so that chords associated with certain keys are close together. One usually plays by pressing the chord buttons with the fingers of the left hand while strumming with a pick held in the right hand.

Next are diagrams showing the placement of the three most important autoharp chords in the keys of C, G, F, A minor, and G minor. Fingering is suggested.

Twelve-bar autoharp

Gm Min.		A⁷ Sev.		Dm Min.		E⁷ Sev.		Am Min.		D⁷ Sev.	
	Bb Maj.		C⁷ Sev.		F Maj.		G⁷ Sev.		C Maj.		G Maj.

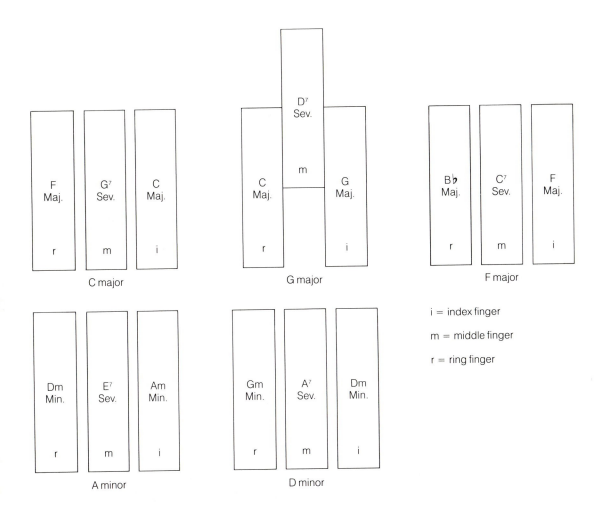

C major

F Maj.	G⁷ Sev.	C Maj.
r	m	i

G major

C Maj.	D⁷ Sev. m	G Maj.
r		i

F major

B♭ Maj.	C⁷ Sev.	F Maj.
r	m	i

i = index finger

m = middle finger

r = ring finger

A minor

Dm Min.	E⁷ Sev.	Am Min.
r	m	i

D minor

Gm Min.	A⁷ Sev.	Dm Min.
r	m	i

Strumming is done rhythmically. Initially, students should be encouraged to use large motions, sweeping across all the strings to a steady beat. Once this style of strumming has been mastered, other patterns can be learned.

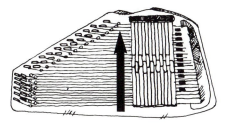

Direction and path of strum

Simple Accompaniment Patterns

Children can create waltz accompaniments by strumming the lower strings of the autoharp (or the lowest string on fretted instruments) on the first beat and higher strings on the second and third beats of each measure.

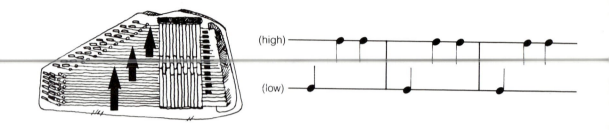

Strums 1–2–3

An accompaniment for duple meter results from an adaptation of the above pattern:

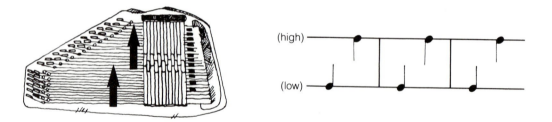

Strums 1–2

Eventually, children can invent their own accompaniment patterns for familiar songs.

Playing an Autoharp with Singing

The development of an ability to accompany children's singing doesn't require years of practice and study. Within an hour you can learn to accompany a number of songs on the autoharp. If you learn the following songs and follow the suggestions, you will find yourself becoming increasingly comfortable as an autoharp player.

Preliminary Practice Suggestions

1. Sing the song.

2. Strum the designated chords with long sweeps. (Small arrows on the music indicate strums.)

3. Sing and strum.

4. Practice the song-starting techniques given with the song.

The first songs can be accompanied by a single chord. "Little Tom Tinker" and "Scotland's Burning" are appropriate for primary grade children. "Shalom Chaverim" is suitable for grades five and six.

Little Tom Tinker

Key: C
Starting note: C (do)

Lit - tle Tom Tink - er got burned with a clink-er* and He be - gan to cry,_____

Ma_____ Ma_____ What a poor fel - low am I.

↑ = strum
*A clinker is a hot coal.

Starting Technique

1. Strum C chord (tonic chord).

2. Sound starting pitch: C.

3. Sing and strum:

Sing: One, two, read - y, sing.

Scotland's Burning

Traditional

Key: F
Starting note: C (sol)

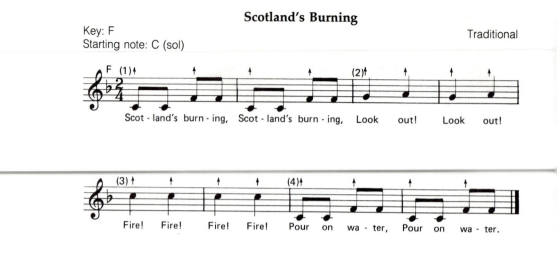

Scot - land's burn - ing, Scot - land's burn - ing, Look out! Look out!

Fire! Fire! Fire! Fire! Pour on wa - ter, Pour on wa - ter.

Starting Technique

1. Strum F chord (tonic chord).

2. Sound starting pitch: C.

3. Sing and strum:

Sing: One, two, read - y, sing.

Shalom Chaverim

Israel

Key: D minor
Starting note: A (mi)

[Musical notation: D min, 4/4 time]

Sha - lom cha - ve - rim! Sha - lom cha - ve - rim! Sha - lom, sha - lom, Le -

[Musical notation]

hit - ra - ot, le - hit - ra - ot, Sha - lom, sha - lom.

Starting Technique

1. Strum D minor chord (tonic chord).

2. Sound starting pitch: A.

3. Sing and strum:

Sing: One, read - y, sing.

The following carol from Colombia requires only two chords for its accompaniment. It can be used in grades three through six.

Little Shepherds
(Vamos, Pastorcitos)

Key: F
Starting note: C (sol)

Colombia

1. Lit-tle shep-herds, leave now,   Go to Beth - le - hem!.
2. For the tin - y In - fant,   Who was born   this day,
3. Lit-tle shep - herds, leave now,   Tra - vel to   a - dore

You will   see   the Vir - gin,   And her tin - y   Son.
You must of - fer   sing - ing,   As by Him   you stay.
Christ, the King   of Heav - en,   At the sta - ble door.

1. Vamos, pastorcitos.
   Vamos a Belén!
   A ver a la Virgen y‿
   Al Niño también.

2. Al pequeño Niño
   Que ha nacido ya,
   Con alegres cantos
   Vamos a arrullar.

3. Vamos, pastorcitos,
   Vamos a adorar
   La Rey de los Cielos
   Que está en el portal.

Starting Technique

1. Strum F chord (tonic chord).

2. Sound starting pitch: C.

3. Sing and strum:

Sing: One read- y sing

Here is a good two-chord song for singing and strumming for upper-grade children.

Down in the Valley

Key: G
Starting note: D (sol)

U.S.

1. Down in the val - ley, the val - ley so low, Hang your head o - ver, hear the winds
2. Build me a cas - tle, for - ty feet high, So I can see him, as he rides

blow. Hear the winds blow, dear, hear the winds blow, Hang your head o - ver, hear the winds blow.
by. As he rides by, dear, as he rides by, So I can see him, as he rides by.

Starting Technique

1. Strum G chord (tonic chord).

2. Sound starting pitch: D.

3. Sing and strum:

Sing: One, two, three, read - y, sing.

Here is a three-chord song suitable for children in grades four to six:

Blackeyed Susie

Key: F
Starting note: C (sol)

U.S.

1. All I want in this cre - a - tion, pret - ty lit - tle wife and a big plan - ta - tion
2. All I need to make me hap - py, wife — and a bab - y to call me pap - py,

Fox in the hol - ler, dog in the wat - er, I'm in love with E - li - ja's daught - er.
Love my — wife and love my — bab - y, Love my dar - ling — black - eyed lad - y.

Hey you pret - ty lit - tle black - eyed Sus - ie, Oh you pret - ty lit - tle black - eyed Sus - ie,

Hey you pret - ty lit - tle black - eyed Sus - ie, Oh you pret - ty lit - tle Sue.

Starting Technique

1. Strum F chord (tonic chord).

2. Sound starting pitch: C.

3. Sing and strum:

Sing: One, two, read - y, sing.

Tips for Strumming Fretted Instruments

Ukuleles and guitars attract older children. The guitar is a standard instrument in the "pop culture," and some of its glamor rubs off on its smaller and less complex cousin, the ukulele.

Guitars and ukuleles can be tuned to a C major chord. (See pp. 257–261 for tuning and chord charts.) This enables children to strum the open strings and have an instantly successful experience. Learning-disabled and some mentally retarded students can participate in these strumming activities. A little assistance from the teacher will help them produce steady strumming motions.

Guitar tuned to C

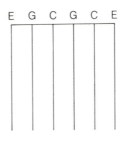

Ukulele tuned to C

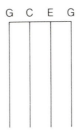

Melodies such as "Row, Row, Row Your Boat," "Three Blind Mice," and "Little Tom Tinker" can be accompanied by rhythmic strumming on the C chord.

If two guitars are available, songs requiring two chords can also be played (see Appendix B). Tune one guitar to the C chord and the other to a G chord.

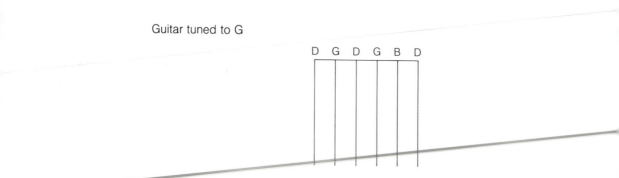

Guitar tuned to G

D G D G B D

After one child plays the C chord and another the G chord, they can alternate to accompany two-chord songs.

Children in fifth and sixth grades enjoy the challenge of learning the fingerings for a few chords.* The simplest of the fretted instruments is the ukulele, and the most versatile member of that family is the baritone uke. The baritone uke has more resonance than the smaller soprano uke and can be used effectively to accompany slow and lyrical songs as well as those that are vigorous. The soprano uke is at its best with bright, spirited music.

PLAYING WIND INSTRUMENTS

Recorders provide children with a means of playing melodies. They can also serve as a concrete adjunct to the music reading program. Generally, by the age of nine a child has the hand size, finger length, and coordination to cope with covering and uncovering the openings on soprano recorders.

Some schools provide **wind instruments.** If yours does not, you or your children must purchase instruments. Whatever the situation, be sure that each instrument has a tag identifying its current user. School-owned wind instruments must be sterilized for each new or different user.

Soprano recorder

---

*Charts including tuning and fingering of basic chords for guitar and soprano and baritone uke are found on pages 257–261.

How Tones Are Produced

In the first lessons, children should learn good tone production. First, without the instruments, children should practice blowing lightly as though trying to keep a tiny feather in the air. Then they transfer this technique to the instrument as they blow into the mouthpiece of the instrument while fingering the first pitch. Tones should be initiated with a soft *dhoo*, with tongues touching lightly behind the upper front teeth to form the *dh*. Light blowing produces the more beautiful sounds.

Simple Exercises and Melodies

The following diagram shows the basic left-hand fingering for pitches B, A, and G on the soprano recorder. The thumb, which covers the opening on the back of the instrument, is indicated by the letter *T; 1* represents the index finger, *2* is the middle finger, and *3* is the ring finger.

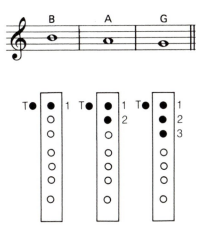

The following songs can be played with these pitches—G, A, and B.

Hot Cross Buns

Traditional

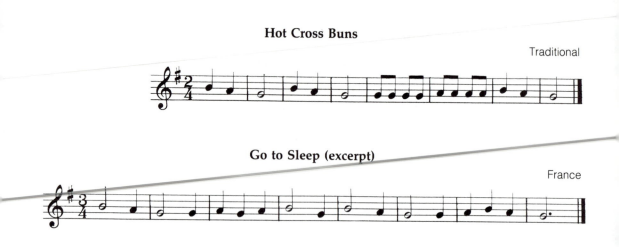

Go to Sleep (excerpt)

France

Here are two more pitches, also involving left-hand fingering.

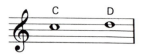

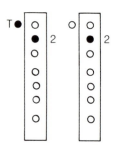

The following songs can be played using the five pitches G, A, B, C, and D.

Lightly Row

Traditional

When the Saints Go Marching In

U.S.

Go Tell Aunt Rhody

U.S.

The song, "London Bridge" on page 20 in Chapter Three and the folk melodies on page 220 in Chapter Thirteen are more songs that can be played with these pitches.

Here are four more pitches that involve both left and right hands.*

---

*The lower pitches on the recorder are the most difficult to play. Players must be absolutely sure the openings that should be covered are completely covered, and they must blow very lightly on the low D and C.

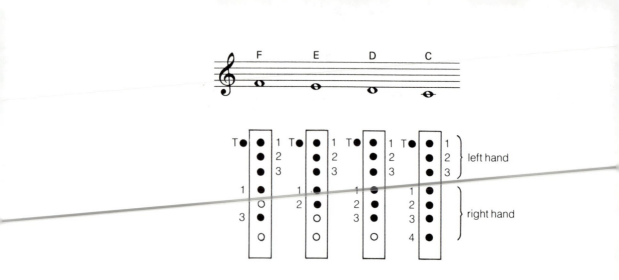

Here is a familiar melody that incorporates these new pitches.

Twinkle, Twinkle, Little Star

Traditional

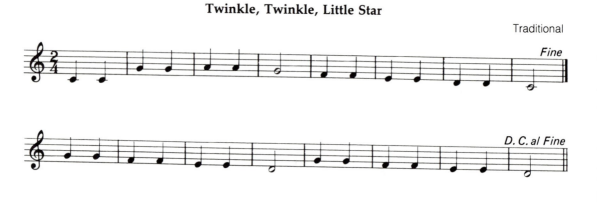

Gradually, children can learn more pitches and fingerings and play many songs and descants from their textbooks, especially with the help of the next figure.

Complete range and fingerings for the soprano recorder

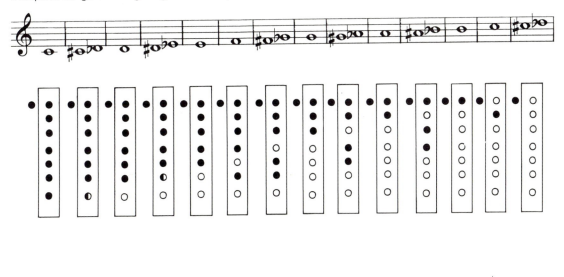

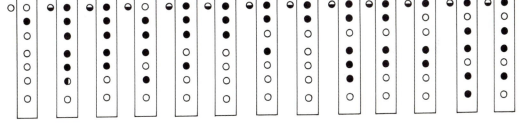

Further attention is given to instrumental activities in Chapter Thirteen. That chapter deals specifically with instruments in the music reading program.

SUMMARY

Classroom instruments can provide accompaniments for songs, help develop musical concepts, and be used for children's improvisations. These instruments belong to three basic categories: percussion, strumming, and wind. Use of instruments will be more effective if orderly guidelines for instrumental activities are established: (1) special routines for setting up and putting away instruments, (2) clear signals for starting and stopping, and (3) assurance that all children have an equal opportunity to play. All children, including mainstreamed students, can benefit from playing instruments.

Preparation for the use of glockenspiels, xylophones, metallophones, and small timpani should include body movements. Two-mallet technique is most easily developed when preceded by appropriate patsching activities.

Strumming instruments can be used to accompany classroom singing. Though guitars and ukuleles may be used, the autoharp is the simplest strumming instrument to play and the most frequently available for school use. You can learn to play the autoharp in a short period of time.

The soprano recorder can be used effectively to provide children with a means of performing melodies. Good tone production should be established in the first lessons.

SUGGESTED PROJECTS

1. Make three different kinds of percussion instruments to use with your classmates. Plan to share the instruments with your future students.

2. Look at a music series textbook, grade of your choice, and make a list of songs that can be accompanied with the two chords C and G.

3. Prepare a collection of songs suitable for playing on the recorder. Organize the songs in order of increasing difficulty.

PART THREE

Developing Musical Understanding

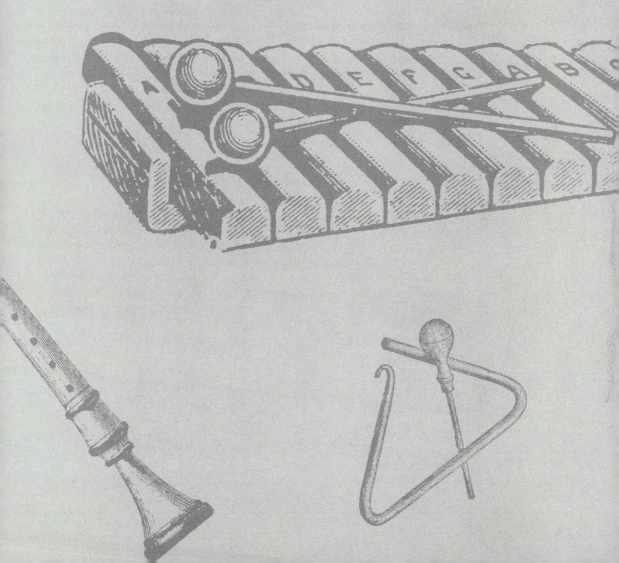

The deepest enjoyment of any form of artistic expression comes with an understanding of its structure. Therefore, Chapters Five through Nine of this book include basic concepts and activities designed to help you, the teacher, and your future students understand the elements of music: *sound*, sensations perceived aurally (through hearing); *rhythm*, arrangements of sounds and silences in time; *melody*, the sequential arrangement of musical tones; *harmony*, the simultaneous presence of two or more tones; and *form*, the pattern or design of musical thoughts or ideas in a composition.

Part Three is organized with separate chapters for each element of music. A set of concepts—abstract thoughts or ideas based on the fundamental characteristics of the musical element—is included with each chapter. Activities, which are presented in two tracks, follow the introduction of each concept or related group of concepts. The first track, *Activities for Teachers*, is designed to reinforce the teacher's understanding of the musical concepts. The second track, *Activities for Children*, contains materials and ideas that will help you teach these concepts.

CONCEPT DEVELOPMENT

The process of concept development includes three general stages: *aural perception*, the processing of sounds through the ear; *accommodating*, the process of integrating, changing, or enlarging information in the brain; and *transferring*, the application of previous learning to new situations. Aural perception and transferring are initiated by the teacher in directed activities (e.g., group singing, playing, moving, and creating). Accommodating is an internal mental process in which new learning is integrated with information previously stored in the brain.

The following figure is a visual representation of the three stages of concept development.

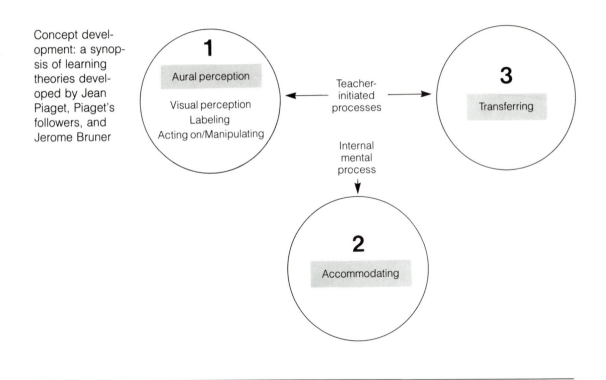

Concept development: a synopsis of learning theories developed by Jean Piaget, Piaget's followers, and Jerome Bruner

1

Aural perception

Visual perception
Labeling
Acting on/Manipulating

Teacher-initiated processes

3

Transferring

Internal mental process

2

Accommodating

AURAL PERCEPTION

All learning begins with perception through one or more of the senses. Musical learning begins with and centers around aural perception, the processing of sounds received by the ear. Before aural perception can occur, the student must focus attention on individual sounds. Because we are surrounded by sounds every day, we may tune out or ignore many of the sounds in our environment. You, as a teacher, can inhibit tuning out in your classroom by directing children's attention to specific elements of music. This effort can be facilitated, and aural perception enhanced, through use of visual perception, acting on and manipulation, and labeling.

Visual Perception

Visual perception (the processing of visual images) plays a supporting role in the aural perception stage of concept development. **Icons** (pictorial representations of musical sounds or sequences) and traditional musical notation reinforce aural perception, as shown in this illustration.

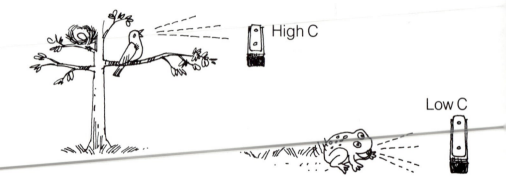

This visual representation of a bird *high* in a tree and a frog *low* on the ground reinforces aural perception of high and low sounds.

Acting On and Manipulating

Acting on and manipulating activities (hands-on experiences) also reinforce aural perception. Children need many opportunities to manipulate and experiment with musical sounds and sound production. This can be accomplished in many ways. As an example, children can express the concept of high and low sounds through movement, stretching their bodies and arms upward for higher pitches and lowering their bodies and arms for lower pitches. They can stand up and sit down; they can point to the ceiling and to the floor; and, of course, they can reproduce high and low pitches with voices or instruments.

Labeling

Labeling associates children's musical experiences with symbols and terminology. This process of attaching labels provides students with another way of thinking about and referring to musical experiences. In the example of high and low sounds, the introduction and use of the terms *high* and *low* enable children to discuss and reflect on their experiences with high and low sounds.

ACCOMMODATING

When a student has perceived, acted on, manipulated, and labeled, the new learning is stored in the brain, changing and enlarging the previous arrangement of information to accept and use the new information. This process is referred to as *accommodating* or accommodation. The new understanding of sound relationships and the musical connotations of the symbols and terminology are integrated with previously stored concepts.

TRANSFERRING

The recognition, identification, or application of previous learning in a new or different presentation or format is called *transferring*. There are many ways in which transferring can be accomplished in the classroom. As an example, children can be asked to (1) locate the highest sound in an unfamiliar song, (2) add high or low sound effects to a story, or (3) select the lowest sound of a group of three sounds. In each case, the students must identify the previous learning as it appears in a new presentation or apply the previous learning to a new situation.

CONCEPT DEVELOPMENT IN THE CLASSROOM
MUSIC PROGRAM

The three stages of concept development (aural perception, accommodating, and transferring) are a vital part of the classroom music program. Long- and short-range planning (see Part Four, Planning for Teaching) involve careful consideration of each of the three stages. When you begin to collect and organize songs and activities for your classroom, you will sequence these activities in a way that will allow students to perceive, accommodate, and transfer selected musical concepts.

Concept Development in Chapters Five through Nine

Activities in Chapters Five through Nine emphasize the aural perception and transferring stages of concept development. As an aid to the teacher, children's activities are grouped under the headings *Aural Perception* and *Transfer*. Most of these activities include opportunities for physical involvement in sound and sound production. Some use icons and traditional music notation as visual reinforcement. Appropriate grade levels, in parentheses, are listed with each activity.

FIVE

Sound

For those of us who hear, sounds fill the world. Even if our external environment is silent, we are still surrounded by the sounds of our bodies functioning. In a quiet room, the sound of our own heartbeats and breathing can seem very loud indeed.

Sound is the basis for speech, a major form of communication between humans. Our hopes, ideas, and most intimate thoughts are communicated through speech. Musical sounds are an additional means of enhancing and expressing thoughts, moods, and feelings.

The characteristics of sound fall into four categories: (1) **pitch** (highness or lowness), (2) **dynamic level** (loudness or softness), (3) **timbre** (tone color or tone quality), and (4) **duration** (length of sounds). Music is composed of sounds with different pitches, dynamics, timbres, and durations. This chapter presents a set of concepts and activities designed to help you and your students explore sounds. The concepts and activities are presented in a sequence that moves from the simple to the more complex and from the concrete to the more abstract. A similar sequence is appropriate in the elementary school classroom.

A number of concepts are basic to understanding sounds in music, as well as all other sounds. These concepts are introduced in most current music series and represent a minimum program in the sound concept area. Each of the concepts, along with appropriate activities for teachers and children, is introduced in the following pages. The development of an awareness of sounds and sound characteristics, plus the acquisition of a vocabulary that can be used to describe those characteristics, forms a solid basis for further musical learning.

CONCEPTS: KINDS OF SOUNDS

- There are many sounds around us.
- Sounds can be described with words such as loud, soft, high, low, short, long.
- Different sources of sound produce sounds with distinct characteristics or tone colors.

Activities for Teachers

1. Experiment with a variety of body sounds (hand claps, tongue clicks, finger snaps, etc.). How many different short sounds can you make? How many different soft sounds can you make? How many loud sounds can you make?

2. Experiment with materials you have at hand (such as notebooks, books, paper, pencils, and pens). How many different kinds of sounds can you make (scraping, rattling, striking, etc.)?

3. Using a set of melody bells or a keyboard instrument as a guide, check the range of your singing voice. What is the highest pitch you can sing? What is the lowest pitch you can sing? (Notice that you move to the right on the bells or keyboard to produce higher pitches and to the left to produce lower pitches.)

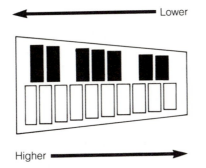

4. Experiment with classroom percussion instruments. Find ways to produce sounds to fit these descriptions: long, short, high, low, soft, loud,

smooth, scratchy, twangy (e.g., long tones on triangles, short tones on sticks, scratchy sounds with sand blocks).

5. Here is a short sound composition with a symbol key to help you interpret the notation. With three of your classmates, develop a performance of the composition with any appropriate sound sources.

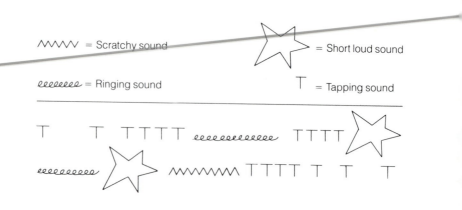

6. Work in a small group to create a 30- to 45-second composition using any sound sources you wish. Try to use different pitches, timbres, dynamics, and durations. Invent your own system of notation for your composition. Give it to a classmate to see if it can be played properly from your notation.

Activities for Children

Aural Perception

1. (Grades K–1) Prepare a sound carrel or corner containing various soundmakers that can be used by young children individually. Ask children to match soundmakers according to timbre, dynamics, or pitch. As an example, your carrel might contain three sets of sand blocks, one with coarse sandpaper and two with fine sandpaper. Ask children to place the sand blocks making *like* sounds on one side, the one that is different on the other. Or place three bells in the area, two of which produce the same pitch. (Bells should be the same size and color.) Ask the children to place the two with identical pitches in a specific location.

2. (Grades K–6) Ask your children to close their eyes and listen carefully, noticing any sounds they hear. For several seconds let them listen to the natural sounds in the environment; then add a few sounds by doing such things as taking a step, rustling a paper, or moving a book across a desk. At the end of 30 seconds, signal the children to open their eyes. Make a list together of the sounds they heard. (You might repeat this activity in a different environment.)

3. (Grades K–6) Tap an object with a small mallet. Invite volunteers to find different sounds by striking other objects with the mallet. Later, discuss the sounds, focusing on timbre, dynamics, and duration.

4. (Grades K–6, depending on the instruments used) If instruments are available, explore all the sounds that can be produced by each instrument. Invite a child to make a sound on an instrument; then ask another child to try to make a different sound with the same instrument.

5. (Grades K–6) Hold a set of melody bells in a vertical position with the lowest bell on the bottom. Using the terms *high* and *low*, compare and discuss the sounds made by striking the lowest and highest bells.

6. (Grades K–6) Using various pitched instruments, play guessing games in which children are asked to identify the highest or lowest sound in a short sequence.

7. (Grades 3–6) Play sounds on instruments such as autoharp, recorder, percussion instruments, piano, or guitar. Listen and describe the sounds.

8. (Grades 3–6) Compare vocal sounds (speaking and singing) in song recordings with teachers' and children's voices. Compare pitches and timbres. Listen and describe.

9. (Grades 2–6) Ask children to find ways to make sounds that fit these descriptions: long, short, high, low, soft, loud, smooth, scratchy, ringing, twangy.

Transfer

1. (Grades 3–6) Older children might be asked to make a sound diary. Include the sounds heard in the classroom, at home, in a store, or on a walk. Children could include descriptions of the sounds. Write the assignment or record it on tape.

2. (Grades 2–4) Plan an experiment with sounds produced by tapping glasses or blowing across openings of bottles. Ask children to compare pitches when the bottles or glasses are empty, partially filled, and completely filled. Ask: When do they make the lowest pitch? When do they make the highest pitch? [Note: This set of experiments could be done in a music corner.]

3. (Grades 2–4) Stretch a rubber band between two hands. Ask children to observe the differences in the breadth of vibrations when the band is stretched tightly and then less tightly. Listen to the pitch changes.

4. (Grades 4–6) Experiments with multiple-speed tape recorders produce interesting results. Invite children to record sounds at one speed; then play them back at another.

CONCEPTS: SOUNDS AND MOOD

After an understanding of the presence and nature of sound has been developed, focus on the expressive qualities of sound, the ways in which sounds communicate feelings and enhance moods.

- A sound can tell us something. Sounds are expressive.
- Sounds can enhance the mood of a poem or story.

Activities for Teachers

1. Make a list of everyday sounds that immediately evoke specific images, thoughts, or reactions (e.g., ambulance, siren, church bells).

2. In a small group, put together a short story or brief account of an event. Plan a sound background that will help tell the story or enhance its moods. Perform it for your classmates. Here is the beginning of such a story.

A Picnic

We got out of the vehicle (close a book sharply to imitate sound of closing door) with our paper bags filled with food (rustle sheets of paper). After deciding which path to take, we set out toward a level area near the water (make stepping sounds with feet). I was holding my bag of food so high I couldn't see my feet, and I tripped over a rock and fell down (slam book on desk), causing the bag to rip (tear sheet of paper). Fortunately, the food wasn't completely demolished; so my friends and I picked up the wrapped sandwiches (rustle paper) and the jars of pickles and olives (tap desk with pen) and walked on (feet make stepping sounds).

3. Listen to compositions such as ''Clair de Lune'' by Debussy (*Bowmar Orchestral Library*, Volume 52), ''Prelude to Act III'' of *Lohengrin* by Wagner (*Adventures in Music*, Grade 6, Volume 1), or ''Flight of the Bumblebee'' by Rimsky-Korsakov (*Bowmar Orchestral Library*, Volume 52) and discuss the moods created by the composers.

Activities for Children

Aural Perception

1. (Grades K–3)   Based on children's input, make a list of ordinary sounds. Discuss what each sound represents. Here is a sample list:
- **a.** alarm clock buzzer (time to get up)
- **b.** dog growling (frightened or angry dog)
- **c.** thunder (storm is nearby)
- **d.** siren (fire or accident)
- **e.** knock at door (someone is there)

2. (Grades 4–6)   Get acquainted with a recording of orchestral music that is descriptive (e.g., "Cloudburst" from Grofe's *Grand Canyon Suite* [*Bowmar Orchestral Library*, Volume 61] or "Hoe Down" from Copland's *Rodeo* [*Adventures in Music*, Grade 5, Volume 2]). Plan a presentation for your class that includes: (1) a discussion of the title and the mood it implies, (2) listening to the recording, and (3) a discussion of the way in which the music expresses the event or mood suggested by the title.

Transfer

1. (Grades 3–6)   Invite children to create a sound background for a poem such as "Hist Whist" by e.e. cummings or "The Fourth" from Shel Silverstein's *Where the Sidewalk Ends*. Let them use vocal or body sounds— or any other soundmakers. Ask the children to develop their own notation and score for their composition.

2. (Grades K–6)   Ask your children to make up a story and accompany it with appropriate sounds. Small children might consider a story about a trip to a zoo, the circus, or a recent field trip.

CONCEPT: TIMBRE

Next, we focus on the tone colors produced by various instruments.

- Each kind of musical instrument produces a sound with a unique tone color or **timbre.**

Because tone color is an important aspect of instrumental music, you and your children need to be able to identify the tone colors of various musical instruments. The following activities provide experiences that develop this ability.

Activities for Teachers

1. If you have instruments available, listen to the same pitch on a recorder, a xylophone, a glockenspiel, and a hand bell. Try to describe the tone quality of each instrument.

2. Listen to the recordings of several songs from a series textbook and try to identify the instruments you hear in the accompaniment. If you have difficulty, check the information in the teacher's edition or on the record jacket and try to match each instrument listed with its sound.

3. Obtain a list of music programs being presented by local colleges, universities, public schools, or musical organizations. Attend instrumental concerts and recitals. Take advantage of any opportunity to hear and see musical instruments.

4. Consult the card catalog of the record library at your school or public library and note the various albums that demonstrate the instruments of the orchestra. If you are unfamiliar with the sounds of some of the orchestral instruments, check out an album and listen to those instruments until you become more familiar with their tone qualities.

Activities for Children

Aural Perception

1. (Grades 2–3)   After children have participated in some of the activities suggested on pages 82–83, organize a guessing game.
   a. Select a song with a repeated and distinctive rhythm pattern such as "Bingo."

Bingo

U.S.

b. Obtain several instruments (e.g., sticks, drums, triangles, and tambourines).

c. Ask children to cover their eyes, sing the song, and listen during the B–I–N–G–O passages.

d. Play the B–I–N–G–O passages on one of the instruments and have the children identify that instrument while their eyes are covered.

e. Repeat the procedure with a different instrument.

f. After each instrument has been identified, lead the children to agree that this recognition is possible because each instrument has its own individual sound or timbre.

2. (Grades K–6, depending on suitability of the music selected) Have children listen to a familiar melody played in the same key on two or three different melody instruments. Notice the difference in the sound produced by each. (If there is an instrumental music program in your school, you might invite children who play trumpet, violin, and flute or clarinet to demonstrate their instruments for your class.)

3. (Grades K–6) If you have a xylophone and a metallophone in your room, ask your children to play and compare the sounds of the pitch C played on both instruments. Compare the sounds produced by blowing across the top of a soft drink bottle with those made by tapping a water glass.

4. (Grades K–4) Share some recordings with your children that feature sounds of different instruments. Prokofiev's "Peter and the Wolf" (Holt, Rinehart & Winston: *Exploring Music,* Grade 1), for narrator and orchestra, is a delightful music story that appeals to children of many ages. "Tubby the Tuba," "Pan the Piper" (both available on commercial recordings), and "Brother John and the Village Orchestra" (Bowmar Records Multi-Media Set #1849) also combine narration and instrumental music in such a way that children follow a story, hear instrumental sounds, and have the sounds identified for them. (It would be helpful for you to have some pictures of various instruments for children to see as they listen to these recordings.)

Transfer

(Grades K–6) As children listen to the recordings of familiar songs from series textbooks, ask them to identify as many of the accompanying instruments as possible.

SUMMARY

Sounds are all around us. Sound is the basis for speech. Musical sounds provide an additional means of communicating thoughts, moods, and feelings.

Music is composed of sounds with different pitches, dynamics, timbres, and durations. In this chapter, teachers and children compare and describe these sounds with words such as high and low, loud and soft, short and long, and scratchy and twangy. They explore the expressive qualities of sound through sound stories and compositions that are descriptive in nature. Finally, they listen to, discuss, and compare the unique tone qualities of musical instruments.

SUGGESTED PROJECTS

1. Read one book on sound appropriate for inclusion in an elementary school library. Review the book, covering (a) age level for which it is suitable, (b) overall appeal for children, (c) adequacy of information presented, (d) possible use in the classroom, and (e) special features.

2. Plan a sound carrel or corner that would be appropriate in a regular classroom. Draw a picture of this carrel or corner. List necessary materials and purchase prices.

3. Compare the approaches to the study of sound presented in the teacher's edition of *Silver Burdett MUSIC* (Grade One) and a Grade One teacher's edition of another recent textbook series. Comment on the quality of the materials and activities presented in each text and on the clarity of the teaching suggestions.

4. Make an annotated list of films and filmstrips that deal with sound in a way that is appropriate for children. Include (a) scope of coverage, (b) possible uses in the classroom, (c) recommended grade or age level, and (d) location or address where the films or filmstrips can be obtained.

5. Create a sound recording on a cassette tape. Collect sounds that carry distinct messages (e.g., telephone ringing, rain falling, faucet dripping, doorbell, footsteps, sweeping with a broom).

6. Compare the approaches to the study of timbre presented in the teacher's editions of at least two second-grade series texts. Based on your findings, select the text you believe you could use most effectively in your own classroom.

7. Make a list of compositions that feature individual musical instruments. Consult current series texts or listening libraries.

SIX

Rhythm in Music

In a factory someone is operating a machine that stamps designs on pieces of metal at regular intervals. In a room somewhere, a father rocks his child to sleep—back and forth, back and forth. At night in a large city, a neon sign is changing its format and color—red, white, red, white. At the seashore, the waves are rolling in, cresting and breaking with some sort of regularity. These events occur in time, each with its own rhythm.

Music also occurs in time and has its own rhythms. **Rhythm** is the aspect of music that pertains to *the progression of sounds and silences in time.* It is rhythm that most frequently elicits a physical response. Our hands clap, toes tap, fingers snap, and heads nod because rhythm makes us feel like moving. Because of this ability to cause response, rhythm is sometimes referred to as the life force in music.

This chapter includes listening, singing, playing, moving, and creating activities that will help you and your children explore rhythm. The concepts presented—beat, meter, rhythm pattern, and syncopation—are basic to an understanding of rhythm and are included in most series textbooks. They represent a minimum program in the rhythm concept area.

CONCEPTS: BEAT AND TEMPO

- Some music has a steady **beat** or pulse. Some music has no feeling of a steady beat or pulse.

- Beats move at different rates of speed. The speed of the beat is referred to as **tempo**.

The ability to perceive the presence or absence of a steady beat in music is crucial to the ability to understand the total rhythmic structure of a musical composition. Therefore it is important that students begin to take part in activities that focus on steady beats as early as possible.

Activities for Teachers

1. Make a list of sounds in the environment that recur at regular intervals.
2. Make a list of physical activities that follow a steady beat.
3. Make a list of children's games that involve keeping a steady beat.
4. Practice reciting nursery rhymes or chants while clapping a steady beat (or performing other body sounds or motions).
5. Practice reciting nursery rhymes or chants while maintaining a steady beat on a nonpitched percussion instrument.
6. Practice clapping or playing a steady beat while singing familiar songs.
7. Experiment with the settings on a metronome (a device that produces steady beats at various speeds). Sing a familiar song several times. With each repetition, use a different metronome setting. Discuss the experience and work out a definition of *tempo*.
8. Listen to the following compositions and decide which include a steady beat and which do not.
   a. Partch, "Cloud Chamber Music" (*Silver Burdett MUSIC*, Grade 5)
   b. Vivaldi, "Spring" from *The Seasons* (*Exploring Music*, Grade 3)
   c. Joplin, "The Entertainer" (*Silver Burdett MUSIC*, Grade 4)

Activities for Children

Aural Perception

1. (Grades K–2)   Ask the children to *follow the leader*—imitating the movements or body sounds made by the teacher while reciting a nursery rhyme or chant.

2. (Grades K–2)   Invite the children to tap a steady beat with chopsticks, or take turns playing the steady beat on other nonpitched instruments, while reciting nursery rhymes or chants.

3. (Grades K–3)   Define *pulse*. Talk about things in everyday life that make sounds like a steady beat or pulse (clocks, turn signals, etc.).

4. (Grades K–4)   Discuss ordinary movements we make that follow steady beats.

5. (Grades K–6)   Discuss children's games that involve keeping a steady beat. Ask your children to think of games that do not involve a steady beat.

6. (Grades K–3)   Plan an activity in which children are asked to move to a steady beat played on a percussion instrument. First, invite them to respond to the steady beat played at a slow tempo. Then, ask them to move to the steady beat played at a fast tempo. Discuss each experience and discover that beats can move at different rates of speed. Introduce the term *tempo*.

Transfer

1. (Grades K–6)   Ask the children to clap or play nonpitched instruments, following the steady beat as they sing familiar songs.

2. (Grades 1–6)   Plan a classroom experience based on Activity 8 from Activities for Teachers. Select several recorded compositions, at least one of which does not include a steady beat. Play them (or excerpts) for your children and ask them to decide which have steady beats.

3. (Grades 1–6)   Plan a listening experience in which recordings of two compositions with contrasting tempos are played, such as "Pantomime" (*Adventures in Music,* Grade 1, Volume 1) and "Comedians' Galop" from Kabalevsky's *The Comedians* (*Adventures in Music,* Grade 3, Volume 1). Invite children to move to the music and compare the tempos.

4. (Grades K–2)   Invite children to use body sounds or nonpitched percussion instruments to perform the steady beat indicated by the following icons.

5. (Grades 3–6, earlier if children are working with notation)   Ask children to use body sounds or nonpitched percussion instruments to perform the steady beat indicated by the following notation.

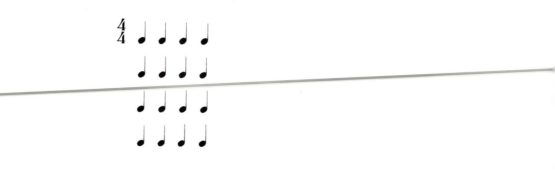

CONCEPT: METER

Once children have developed an ability to perceive and respond to the steady beat in music, you can begin to introduce activities that will enable them to perceive and respond to *beat groupings*.

▪ Steady beats in music can be grouped in twos or threes. These groupings of beats are traditionally referred to as **meter.** The first beat in each group is stressed or accented.

Activities for Teachers

If you have never tried to determine the meter of a musical composition or poem by ear, you may need to develop your meter-sensing* skills. Some of the suggested activities for children may be appropriate for you as an adult before you continue with those presented here.

1. Learn to conduct duple meter (beats grouped in twos). Start with your right hand raised to chin level in front of your body; then let it drop on the first beat until the hand and forearm form a 90-degree angle with the upper arm. Let the hand and forearm bounce slightly; then bring them back up to their original position. Gestures for the right hand are as shown.

Meter sensing is a term often used to refer to the process of determining beat groupings by ear.

Practice conducting in twos while music in duple meter is performed.

2. Learn to conduct in triple meter (beats grouped in threes). The gestures for the right hand are as shown.

Notice that the first beat is indicated with a downward, accented gesture from the same starting position as in duple meter. Practice conducting in threes while music in triple meter is performed.

3. Practice strumming chords on the autoharp in duple and triple meter. Accent the first beat of each grouping.

4. Practice stepping meter. Stamp on the accented beats and step lightly on the unaccented beats as you stand in place or move in a circle:

L r **L** r **L** r (2)
L r l **R** l r **L** r l **R** l r (3)

Activities for Children

Aural Perception

1. (Grades 1–3) Set up a simple body sound sequence in twos, such as

patsch clap, patsch clap, patsch clap

2. (Grades 1–3) Have children patsch and clap a steady beat as they chant:

```
P       c      P      c
One   potato  two  potato
P       c      P      c
Three potato four,
P       c      P      c
Five   potato  six  potato
P       c      P      c
Seven potato more.
```

Set up a simple body sound sequence in threes, such as

patsch clap clap, patsch clap clap, patsch clap clap

Invite the children to perform this pattern as they chant:

```
P          c    c    P    c    c
Je-       re-  my, Jen- ni- fer,
P          c    c    P    c    c
Har-      vey  and  Jo,
P          c    c    P    c    c
Walked down the street but had
P          c    c    P    c    c
No        place to   go.
```

3. (Grades 1–3)   Select two nonpitched percussion instruments or sound-makers with contrasting sounds. Use the instruments to highlight the accented and unaccented beats in accompaniments for appropriate songs or rhymes.

Transfer

(Grades 2–6)   Have the children listen to recordings of instrumental music and determine whether the music is moving in twos:

or in threes:

Encourage the children to make body motions as an aid in feeling the meter before they respond (e.g., patsch–clap, patsch–clap *or* patsch–clap–clap, patsch–clap–clap).

(The use of icons for visual reinforcement and body movements for kinesthetic reinforcement helps learning-disabled students develop their ability to perceive meter.)

CONCEPTS: RHYTHM PATTERN

The steady beat and meter form the framework for arrangements of long and short sounds and silences. In this section you will explore these rhythm patterns.

- Some sounds are long. Some sounds are short.
- *A rhythm pattern* consists of a group, or pattern, of long and short sounds. Some rhythm patterns contain silences (rests).
- Words we use every day form rhythm patterns. When we sing a song, the words and melody form rhythm patterns. When we move across the floor, our feet make sounds that form rhythm patterns.

Activities for Teachers

1. Separate into small groups. In each group, make a list of words that relate to a topic that is studied by younger children (e.g., colors, foods, or animals). Chant the words until they form a set rhythm pattern. Next, clap the rhythm patterns. Verbalize the patterns using the words *short* and *long*. Later, perform the patterns on nonpitched instruments or soundmakers, or with other body sounds. Share your patterns with the class.

   Examples:
   a. robin, sparrow, bluebird, jay
   b. house finch, chickadee, mockingbird, crow

2. Invite a classmate to move around the room. Use body sounds or nonpitched soundmakers to accompany the movement. Encourage each other to be creative and try different kinds of locomotor movements. (This will help you adapt accompaniments to children's movements when you are in your own classroom.)

3. Select a familiar song and find one or two rhythmic **motives** (rhythm patterns that occur two or more times). Separate into groups, one for each motive. Assign a body or instrumental sound to each motive. Sing the song and perform each pattern as it occurs. (This activity is also appropriate for upper grades.)

4. Another interesting percussion accompaniment can be developed by playing several of the rhythmic motives of a song simultaneously. Work in a small group and develop such an accompaniment for a familiar song. Perform it for your class.

Activities for Children

Aural Perception

1. (Grades K–1) Help younger children discover and clap the rhythm patterns of their names. First, chant each name several times. Next, ask the children to "clap the way their names sound." (This is a good reinforcement for the study of syllabification.) Here are two examples:

Speak   *Mar* - y
 clap   X   x
Speak   *Jon* - a - thon
 clap   X x x

2. (Grades K–3) Clear some space for moving and ask for a volunteer to move across the space in any manner. Clap the rhythm pattern of the child's walk or play it on a drum, tambourine, or other nonpitched soundmaker. Repeat the procedure with other children. Encourage individuality. If a child with a manually operated wheelchair volunteers to move across the floor, clap or play the rhythm of the child's arm movements. (It is always best during initial movement activities to allow individuals to establish their own movements and tempos.)

3. (Grades 2–3) Vary Activity 1 by having children play their names on nonpitched percussion instruments or soundmakers. Later, learn "Michael Finnegan" (p. 237) and ask children to clap the name every time they sing it.

4. (Grades 4–6) It is possible to create an interesting sound composition by combining a number of names that form different rhythm patterns. Assign different soundmakers to each pattern and perform them simultaneously.

Transfer

1. (Grades 2–4) Invite children to clap patterns of words and phrases in a familiar song. (Some books refer to these patterns as "the rhythm of the melody" or "the rhythm of the words.") Let children sing and clap a few times; then ask them to clap the song without singing.

2. (Grades 2–4) Play "mystery song." Clap the rhythm pattern of the opening of a song that is familiar to the children. Ask them to identify the song.

3. (Grades 4–6, or earlier if the children are working with notation) When children have had experience with notation, write the rhythm pattern of the opening of a familiar song on the board (or on a chart) and ask them to identify it. You may want to let them answer individually, or ask the children to try to clap the rhythm together.

CONCEPT: COMBINING BEAT, METER, AND RHYTHM PATTERN

Once the elements of rhythm are understood, you are ready to participate in activities that focus on the way in which beat, meter, and rhythm patterns occur simultaneously in music.

▪ Beat, meter, and rhythm patterns combine to form the *rhythmic* element in music.

Activities for Teachers

1. Organize in groups of three or six, and choose a song you can all sing. Divide into three parts (one or two on a part). Each part is responsible for performing an appropriate body sound (nonvocal) to emphasize one aspect of the rhythm of the song you are going to sing: beat, accented beats, or rhythm patterns. Practice singing the song while accompanying it with the body sounds. Perform your song with the accompaniment for the class.

2. Repeat Activity 1, substituting nonpitched instruments for the body sounds.

3. Perform the three aspects of rhythm simultaneously as you sing a familiar song (e.g., "Are You Sleeping" [p. 233] and "Hey, Betty Martin" [p. 227]).
   a. Step the beat.
   b. Dip and stamp the accented beat.
   c. Clap the rhythm patterns.

Activities for Children

Aural Perception

1. (Grades 2–6)   Let the children tap the beat with pens or pencils on their desks while they sing a song that they know well and enjoy. Next, try singing while patsching on the first beat of each group. Finally, let them sing while clapping the rhythm patterns.

2. (Grades 3–6)   On another day, divide the class into three groups. Group I will clap lightly on the steady beat, Group II will patsch the accented beats, and Group III will clap the rhythm patterns, while all sing the song. After they have practiced several times, ask the students to perform the rhythmic elements of the song while singing the song silently "in their heads." Let them discover that they have combined beat, meter, and rhythm patterns—all of the rhythmic elements of music.

Transfer

(Grades 2–6)   Repeat Activity 1, substituting nonpitched soundmakers for body sounds. Be sure that each group is assigned a contrasting sound.

CONCEPT: SYNCOPATION

Syncopation is a special kind of rhythm pattern encountered in all kinds of music—folk, popular, jazz, and classical.

▪ An accent or stress on a beat or a part of a beat not usually stressed creates a rhythmic effect referred to as **syncopation.**

Activities for Teachers

1. Practice chanting the numbers in the following figure to a steady beat, stressing those that are circled. The first and third sets involve the usual accents in duple and triple meter. The second and fourth are syncopated.

(a) ① 2 ③ 4 ⑤ 6 ⑦ 8 (repeat)

(b) 1 ② 3 ④ 5 ⑥ 7 ⑧ (repeat)

(c) ① 2 3 ④ 5 6 ⑦ 8 9 (repeat)

(d) 1 ② 3 4 ⑤ 6 7 8 ⑨ (repeat)

2. Separate into two groups. Group 1 steadily chants the first set of numbers in the following figure, stressing the circled numbers. Group 2 chants the second set of numbers, observing the accents. Decide which set provides an example of syncopation. After each group has practiced its part, chant them together; repeat the exercise several times until you become accustomed to the feel of the syncopation.

(a) ① 2 ③ 4 ⑤ 6 ⑦ 8

   ① 2 ③ 4 ⑤ 6 ⑦ 8

(b) ① 2 3 ④ 5 6 ⑦ 8

   ① 2 3 ④ 5 6 ⑦ 8

3. Repeat Activities 1 and 2, counting softly and using body or percussion sounds to highlight the accents.

4. Learn to sing this American folk song about the legendary hero John Henry. When you can sing it well, emphasize the syncopated rhythm patterns (marked by brackets), clapping them as you sing.

John Henry

1. When John Hen-ry was a lit-tle ba-by sit-ting on his__ pap-py's__
2. John__ Hen-ry said__ to his cap-tain, "A__ man ain't__ noth-in' but a

knee, He__ took a ham-mer and a lit-tle piece of steel, said, "This
man, But be-fore I'll let your steam drill beat__ me__ down, I'll __

ham-mer'll be the death__ of__ me, O Lord,__ this ham-mer'll be the death__ of__ me."
die __ with the ham-mer in my hand! O Lord!__ I'll die __ with the ham-mer in my hand!"

Activities for Children

Aural Perception

1. (Grades 3–6) Invite your children to count steadily from one to eight several times while you clap or play the accents (the circled numbers in this figure).

① 2 ③ 4 ⑤ 6 ⑦ 8 (repeat)

Ask the children to continue their counting while you emphasize different accents (the circled numbers in this figure) in a similar manner.

1 ② 3 ④ 5 6 7 ⑧ (repeat)

Point out that the rhythmic effect created in the second activity is called *syncopation*.

2. (Grades 3–6)   Ask your children to count steadily from one to nine several times while you clap or play the accents (the circled numbers in this next figure).

① 2 3 ④ 5 6 ⑦ 8 9 (repeat)

Then ask them to continue counting while you emphasize different accents (the circled numbers in this figure) in a similar manner.

1 ② 3 4 5 ⑥ 7 ⑧ 9 (repeat)

3. (Grades 3–6)   Teach this calypso song from Jamaica to your children. Point out that the rhythm pattern at the end of each line (in brackets) is syncopated. You can explain this to older children as follows: A short note at the beginning of a metrical group (measure) followed by a long note creates a syncopated rhythm.

Hill and Gully Rider

Jamaica

Transfer

1. (Grades 3–6) Invite children to suggest syncopated body-sound accompaniments for the steady chanting of the numbers one to eight. Here is an example:

1	2	3	4	5	6	7	8	[repeat]
s	C	s	C	s	C	s	C	

(s = finger snap   C = loud clap)

2. (Grades 3–6) Teach a song that contains clear examples of syncopated patterns. Later, invite children to clap the rhythmic patterns as they sing and identify those that are syncopated. "This Train" includes several examples. Each phrase of the melody begins with a syncopated pattern:

This   train   is

Each phrase of the melody also ends with a syncopated pattern:

This   train____

SUMMARY

Rhythm is the aspect of music that pertains to the progression of sounds and silences in time. The components of rhythm are beat, meter, and rhythm patterns. In this chapter, teachers and students develop an awareness of beat by active participation in clapping, stepping, tapping, and playing. They develop their meter-sensing skills through conducting, playing, chanting, and body movements. They explore the rhythm patterns in familiar words, poems, and movements. In the last two sections, beat, meter, and rhythm patterns are combined, and syncopation is introduced.

SUGGESTED PROJECTS

1. Using symbols that depict or represent specific body or hand motions, make a chart for a body-movement or hand-jive* sequence that could be used with the steady beat of a recording of instrumental music. Make the chart large enough for children to see easily.

2. Compare approaches to at least one rhythmic concept found in *Silver Burdett MUSIC, Macmillan Music,* and *The Music Book* (Holt, Rinehart & Winston). Which book presents materials and related activities that you could most easily incorporate in your own teaching?

3. Listen to the instrumental selections included in recordings for one of the elementary series (Grade K or 1) or RCA *Adventures in Music* (Grade 1, Vol. 1). Find at least two compositions in which the meter is obviously duple and at least two in which the meter is obviously triple. Make a list of the compositions and sources to share with your classmates.

4. Select at least five songs that contain syncopated rhythm patterns from an elementary series text for grade five or six. Share the songs with your classmates and point out the examples of syncopation.

---

*A *hand jive* is a movement pattern involving the upper body. It can include clapping hands, snapping fingers, tapping shoulders, head, or other body parts, or clapping hands with another person.

SEVEN

Melody in Music

Do you sometimes hum or whistle while you are engaged in a routine activity? Many of us do. We may be sweeping, raking, hammering, jogging, or walking and a melody lifts our spirits and helps us overcome tedium.

Melody, the sequential arrangement of pitches in time, is one of the basic elements of music. For many of us, it is the most memorable element of the music we love. After attending a musical performance, we may find ourselves humming one of the melodies for the next few days. We are able to do so because we remember how the melody moves. We remember where and when and how much higher or lower it moves. This is the nature of melody: It moves up to higher pitches, down to lower pitches, and sometimes repeats the same pitch several times.

When you and your children acquire a repertoire of several songs, you can begin to focus on melody. As you listen to melodic movement, play short melodies on classroom instruments, look at visual representations of melody, and create your own melodies, you will begin to understand melodic concepts. The following concepts represent a minimum program and are included in most music series texts. In this chapter, each melodic concept is introduced with appropriate activities for teachers and for children.

CONCEPTS: MELODIC DIRECTION

Concepts of melodic direction must be understood before more precise aspects of melodic movement can be perceived.

- Melodies can move *up*.
- Melodies can move *down*.
- Melodies can stay on the *same level*.

Activities for Teachers

1. Use a set of melody bells, step bells, resonator bells, hand bells, or a keyboard instrument and play three four-note melodies: one that moves up, one that moves down, and one that stays on the same level.

2. Listen to short melodies played by your instructor and say or write the direction in which each melody moves.

3. Listen to the endings of the songs in Chapter Fourteen and indicate the direction in which the melody moves.

4. Practice playing melodies with various shapes on bells (i.e., upward, downward, and same); then try to "play the shapes" of objects you see around you. An example is this shape of two sides and the top of a blackboard:

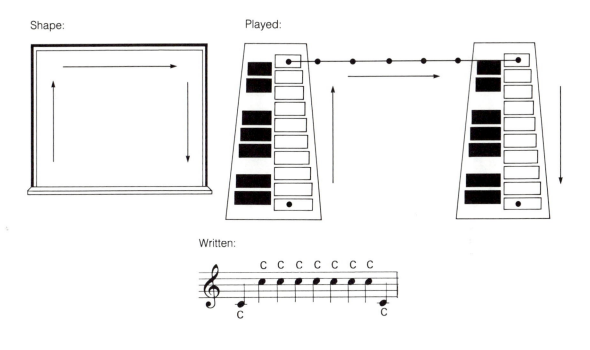

Shape:

Played:

Written:

Activities for Children

Aural Perception

1. (Grades K–2)   Strum the autoharp accompaniment for a song such as "Sing Hello" (p. 20) without singing the melody. Then sing the melody by itself. Ask the children to describe each activity. If children do not supply the term *melody*, point out that when a song is sung, you are singing a melody.

2. (Grades 1–2)   After playing and discussing short examples of melodies moving up, moving down, and staying on the same level, ask children to play short melodies moving in each direction on bells or tuned water glasses.

3. (Grades 2–6, depending on song)   Help children relate the sound of the melodic direction of a passage in a familiar song to icons or standard musical notation, as in the following examples.

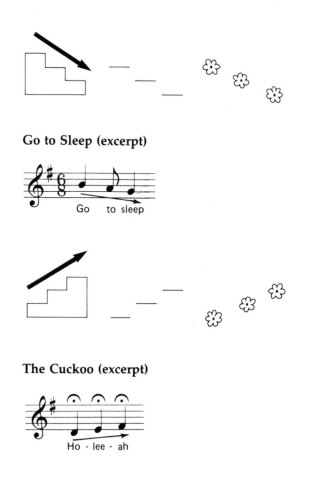

Go to Sleep (excerpt)

Go   to sleep

The Cuckoo (excerpt)

Ho - lee - ah

Sourwood Mountain (excerpt)

My true love she

Transfer

1. (Grades 2–6) Have children identify the melodic direction of short passages in familiar and unfamiliar songs by ear. As an example, ask children to identify the melodic direction of this excerpt from "Sourwood Mountain."

Sourwood Mountain (excerpt)

Sour - wood Moun-tain

2. (Grades 1–2) Play a game in which one child plays a short melody moving in one direction and other children respond with corresponding body motions. For example, one child plays a melody moving up on the bells, and the other children respond by moving their arms toward the ceiling.

3. (Grades 1–2) As a variation of the previous activity, distribute large cards, each of which displays an arrow.

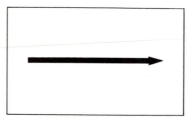

When a short melody is played, children hold their cards in front of their bodies and point the arrow in the corresponding direction.

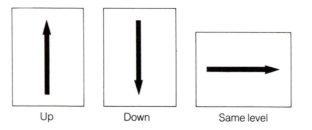

Up   Down   Same level

CONCEPT: MELODIC STEPS AND SKIPS

When you have explored the directions in which melodies can move, you are ready to consider specific ways in which these movements are made.

- Melodies can move up and down by *steps* (tones that are close together) or *skips* (tones that are farther apart).

Activities for Teachers

1. Collect a series of short melodies that move by steps or skips. Perform these melodies on a set of bells, tuned water glasses, or a keyboard instrument.

2. Find short examples of steps and skips in songs in this text and share them with your classmates.

3. Listen to several recorded instrumental selections from music series or listening series albums. Discuss the type of melodic movement most prevalent in each. For instance, you might compare the melodic movement of the opening melody of "Bydlo" from Mussorgsky's *Pictures at an Exhibition* (*Adventures in Music*, Grade 2, Volume 1) with that of the opening melody of "Circus Music" from Copland's *Red Pony Suite* (*Adventures in Music*, Grade 3, Volume 1).

Activities for Children

Aural Perception

1. (Grades K–2)   On bells or tuned water glasses, play examples of short melodies that move by steps and by skips. If you are using melody bells, hold them vertically for visual reinforcement of the melodic movement. Discuss the difference between movement by steps and movement by skips.

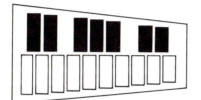

2. (Grades 1–3)   Ask children to identify the movement of short melodies as up or down by steps or skips, or as repeated tones (tones that stay on the same level).

3. (Grades 3–6)   Help children relate the sound of the melodic movement of passages in these familiar songs to icons and notation.

Hop Up! My Ladies (excerpt)

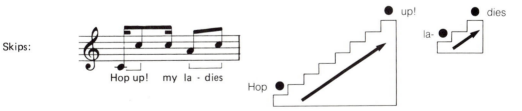

Down by the Station (excerpt)

Steps:

off they go.

● off
● they
● go

Sing Hello (excerpt)

Repeated tones:

Sing hel - lo

Sing hel - lo
● ● ●

Transfer

1. (Grades 2–6) Have children identify the kind of melodic movement found in excerpts from familiar songs.

2. (Grades 2–6) Organize a guessing game. A child is chosen to be *it* and comes to the front of the room (or sits in the middle of a circle). Classmates sit with their eyes closed. *It* plays a short melody on bells or glasses and the first child to identify melodic movement correctly gets to be the next *it*. This game could also be played as a team game (with the teacher playing short melodies).

CONCEPT: SCALES

When you can perceive the differences between steps and skips, it is time to focus on sequences of pitches called **scales.**

- Pitches can be arranged in sequences referred to as *scales. Major* and *minor scales* are sequences that move by steps. *Pentatonic scales* are sequences that contain skips or gaps.

Activities for Teachers

1. Play the white bells from C to C on a set of melody bells: C-D-E-F-G-A-B-C. This is the series of pitches called the C major scale. (Its name is derived from the first note in the series: C.) Notice that the pitches move by steps.

2. Play the white bells from A to A on a set of melody bells (or on a piano): A-B-C-D-E-F-G-A. This series of pitches is called the A minor scale. Notice that it, like the C major scale, moves by steps.

3. Play the following pitches on a set of melody bells: F-G-A-C-D. This series of pitches is called a *pentatonic scale*. Notice that it contains only five pitches and that there is a skip between the third and fourth pitches. These characteristics give pentatonic scales a sound that is quite different from those of major or minor scales.

4. Sing the opening of "Joy to the World," one of the standard Christmas carols.

Joy to the world, the Lord is come.

You have just sung all of the pitches of the C major scale from the highest to the lowest. Notice that the notes are placed in descending order, on consecutive lines and spaces of the staff.

5. Sing "He's Gone Away," an American folk song that is based on a pentatonic scale:

He's Gone Away

U.S.

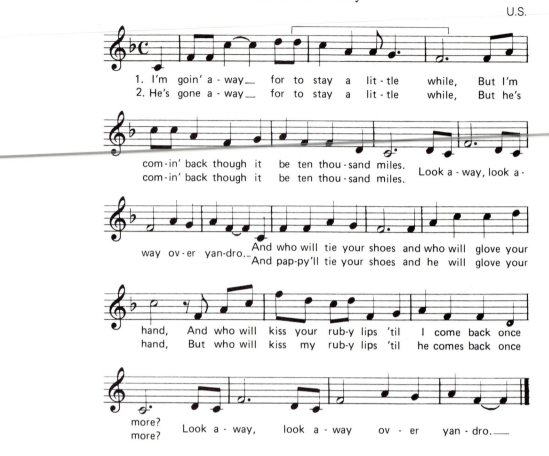

1. I'm goin' a-way__ for to stay a lit-tle while, But I'm
2. He's gone a-way__ for to stay a lit-tle while, But he's

com-in' back though it be ten thou-sand miles.
com-in' back though it be ten thou-sand miles. Look a-way, look a-

way ov-er yan-dro.__ And who will tie your shoes and who will glove your
And pap-py'll tie your shoes and he will glove your

hand, And who will kiss your rub-y lips 'til I come back once
hand, But who will kiss my rub-y lips 'til he comes back once

more? Look a-way, look a-way ov-er yan-dro.__
more?

The passage in brackets outlines a descending pentatonic scale in which one pitch is repeated. Notice the skip between C and A.

Activities for Children

Aural Perception

1. (Grades 2–4) Teach your children "St. Paul's Steeple" by rote.

St. Paul's Steeple

England

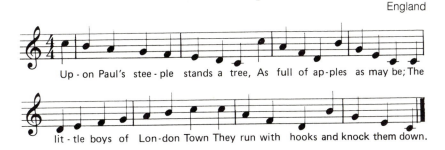

Up - on Paul's stee - ple stands a tree, As full of ap-ples as may be; The

lit - tle boys of Lon-don Town They run with hooks and knock them down.

Play the passage "Upon Paul's steeple stands a tree" on a pitched instrument and ask children to describe how the melody moves (melody moving down by steps). Introduce the term *scale*. Play the sequence from the lowest note up to the highest, pointing out that a scale can be played or sung in either direction: up or down. Ask the children if there is a passage in the song that sounds like an ascending scale ("The little boys of London Town"). Play the scale up and down once again, inviting the children to sing along on a neutral syllable such as *loo*.

2. (Grades 2–6) Invite a volunteer to play the opening passage of "St. Paul's Steeple" on the bells while you guide the attention of the class to an iconic representation of the descending scale.

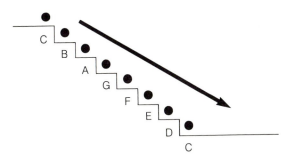

Then invite another volunteer to play the passage "The little boys of London Town" while you guide the attention of the class to an iconic representation of the ascending scale.

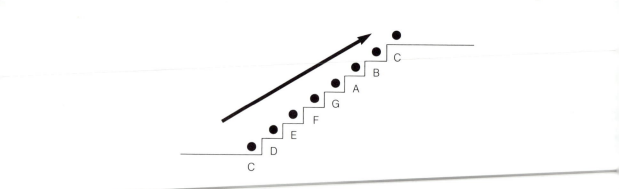

Lead children to discover that the eight notes of both passages move down or up in a series of steps. (The scale passages can be related to music notation by sharing the written version of the song with the children.) You may want to introduce the term *major scale*.

3. (Grades 2–3)   Teach your children "All the Pretty Little Horses."

All the Pretty Little Horses

U.S.

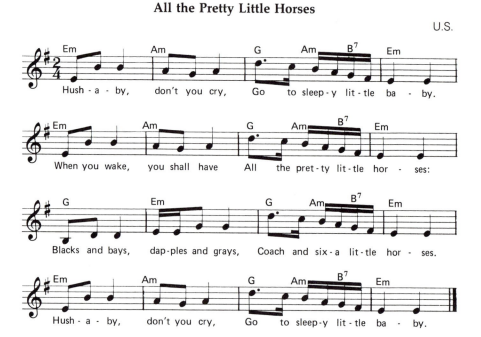

Hush - a - by,   don't you cry,   Go   to sleep-y lit-tle ba - by.

When you wake,   you shall have   All   the pret-ty lit-tle hor - ses:

Blacks and bays,   dap-ples and grays,   Coach and six-a lit-tle hor - ses.

Hush - a - by,   don't you cry,   Go   to sleep-y lit-tle ba - by.

After children can sing the song well, focus on the sound of the descending melodic line:

go   to sleep-y lit-tle ba - by.

Play a descending E major scale on the bells:

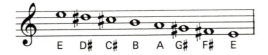

E D♯ C♯ B A G♯ F♯ E

Now play a descending E minor scale:

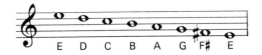

E D C B A G F♯ E

Ask which version sounds most like the melody for "Go to sleepy little baby." (If necessary, leave off the high E.) Remind the children that the first scale you played was a major scale. Explain that the second scale, the one that sounded like the melody of their song, is a minor scale. (If you have been using the tonic chord approach for starting songs, you could point out that the la–do–mi chord is associated with minor scales.)

4. (Grades 3–5)   Teach your children "Goodby, Old Paint" by rote.

Goodby, Old Paint

Play the passage "I'm leavin' Cheyenne" on the bells and explain that it includes the tones of the scale on which the melody of the song is based.

Invite the children to count the number of pitches they hear as you play the passage again. Play the passage for a third time, pointing out the skip between the pitches C and A. Discuss the term *pentatonic*.

5. (Grades 3–5) Ask a volunteer to play the passage from "Goodby, Old Paint" on the bells while you guide the attention of the class to an iconic representation of the descending pentatonic scale.

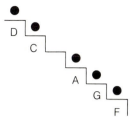

The scale passage could be related to the notation by sharing the written version of the song with the children.

Transfer

1. (Grades 3–6)   Collect enough resonator or hand bells to build a major or minor scale. Invite eight children to come to the front of the room and stand in a line facing the class. Distribute the bells in random order. Tell the class that they are going to arrange the bell players in sequence from the lowest to the highest (or vice versa). Then use this procedure:

   a. Ask players to sound their bells individually.

   b. Class decides whose bell is lowest. That child moves to the left end of the line.

   c. The next seven players sound their bells one at a time.

   d. Class decides whose bell is lowest and asks that child to become the second player from the left.

   e. Repeat the process until all players are in order.

   f. Then ask the children to play in sequence from left to right.

   g. Ask the children to describe what they heard.

   Ask your children to describe what they have created. They should respond with the term *scale*.

2. (Grades 3–5)   Invite a child to play five consecutive black keys on a piano or bells. Discuss and label the scale (pentatonic).

CONCEPT: HOME TONE

Scales are a framework for the melodic structure of music. In this section you will discover that many melodies move away from and return to the first tone of the scale, the **home tone**. The activities presented focus on hearing and identifying the home tone.

- In traditional music of many cultures, melodies generally move away from and return to a *home tone*. A return to the home tone at a melody's end creates a strong sense of completion and relaxation. The home tone is the lowest, or first, note of a scale.

Activities for Teachers

1. Sing several of the songs in Chapter Fourteen. Notice that all end on the home tone.

2. Listen to the following pairs of melodies and decide which of each pair ends on the home tone.

Sur le Pont d'Avignon (excerpt)

My Ball Is Rolling (excerpt)

Ev'rybody Loves Saturday Night (excerpt)

3. Sing a descending major or minor scale with a long pause before you sing the final note (the lowest note of the scale). Notice that you feel a strong sense of completion when you finally sing the home tone.

Developing Musical Understanding

Activities for Children

Aural Perception

1. (Grades 2–4)   Review "St. Paul's Steeple" (p. 113) or another song with a melody that contains a descending scale. Invite the children to sing the first line, stopping just before the word *tree.* Then ask them to add *tree.* Point out that *tree* is sung on the first note of the scale, which is the home tone.

2. (Grades 3–6)   Play or sing both versions of "Michael, Row the Boat." Ask the children which version sounds finished. Indicate that the second version ends on the pitch called the *home tone.*

Transfer

1. (Grades 2–6)   Set up a C major scale with bells or water glasses in a music corner and invite children individually to create a melody for a short saying. For example:

Early to bed and early to rise,

Makes a man healthy, wealthy, and wise.

Establish guidelines:
a. The melody must begin on C and end on C (the home tone).
b. The melody must contain one pitch for each syllable in the text.
Children can notate their melodies by writing the letter names of the pitches in sequence or by using traditional notation.

---

2. (Grades 2–6) Invite your children to supply an ending pitch (vocally or instrumentally) that will make the following melody sound complete. Be sure to point out that this melody does not begin on the home tone.

SUMMARY

Melody is the sequential arrangement of pitches in time. In this chapter, teachers and students explore melodic direction (up, down, and same), melodic movement (steps and skips), scales, and the concept of home tone. The ability to perceive and identify melodic direction and movement is developed through use of melodic instruments, active experimentation with melodic shape, recognition games, and comparison of melodic movement in songs and instrumental compositions. Major, minor, and pentatonic scales are explored through familiar songs and active involvement in scale building. The concept of home tone is explored by comparing the endings of familiar songs and creating melodies.

SUGGESTED PROJECTS

1. Compare the approaches to at least one melodic concept found in *Silver Burdett MUSIC, Macmillan Music,* and *The Music Book.* Discuss the musical materials and activities suggested in each text. Which are most appropriate? Why?

2. Make a cassette recording that includes short examples of accompaniments without melodies, melodies without accompaniments, and rhythm patterns on nonpitched soundmakers. Use the cassette with children as they are learning to distinguish melody from other elements of music.

3. Make a cassette recording of short melodies played on tuned water glasses or bells. Plan to use the recording in a music corner in which individual students can practice playing the melodies.

4. Make a cassette recording of ten short melodies that are played on an instrument familiar to the children. Prepare an evaluation sheet on which they will circle the melodic direction of each melody: up, down, or same. A typical entry on the sheet might look like this:

5. Prepare another evaluation sheet asking children to identify the type of movement in each example: steps, skips, or repeated tones.

EIGHT

*H*armony in Music

Did you ever go to camp? If so, you may recall harmonizing around the campfire. **Harmony,** the result of sounding different pitches at the same time, adds an interesting dimension to music.

Though younger children may have problems with singing harmony parts, they can learn to perceive harmony and create and perform accompaniments for songs on instruments or other soundmakers. Older children can be expected to develop the auditory, vocal, and instrumental skills necessary for singing part songs and playing ostinati (or descants) on pitched instruments.

Through listening, singing, playing, and creating, you and your future students can explore the harmonic dimension of music and develop an understanding of the nature of harmony. The concepts of harmony, which are included in current music series texts, are introduced here with appropriate activities.

CONCEPTS: HARMONY

- Harmony is the sounding of different pitches at the same time.
- Some harmonic textures are **homophonic.** Some harmonic textures are **polyphonic.** A homophonic texture occurs when a melody is combined

with a chordal accompaniment. A **chord** consists of three or more simultaneous pitches. When you press a bar on an autoharp and strum, you are playing a chord. A polyphonic texture occurs when two or more independent melodies are combined.

Activities for Teachers

1. Learn to sing "Canoe Song." Develop a homophonic texture by singing the song with a D-minor chord played on a strumming instrument throughout or with a bordun (drone) played by striking the D and A bells simultaneously on a steady beat.

Canoe Song

Words and music by
Margaret Embers McGee

1. My pad - dle's keen and bright, Flash - ing with sil - ver,
   Dip, dip and swing and back, Flash - ing with sil - ver,

Fol - low the wild goose flight, Dip, dip and swing.
Fol - low the wild goose track, Dip, dip and swing.

2. Create a polyphonic texture by singing "Canoe Song" in two parts. Have one group sing "Dip, dip and swing" as an ostinato while the other group sings the melody.

3. Sing "Canoe Song" as a round. The entrance (as each earlier part reaches a number) of melodies at different times creates another type of polyphonic texture.

4. Create a polyphonic accompaniment for "Canoe Song" on pitched instruments (melody bells, Orff-type mallet instruments). Your accompaniment may include several parts: two or three short melodies, containing the notes C, D, F, G, and A, played continuously as ostinati. Perform the accompaniment while the class sings "Canoe Song."

5. Listen to examples of harmonic textures. The opening of "Barcarolle" from *Tales of Hoffman* by Offenbach (*Adventures in Music*, Grade 3, Volume 1) is an example of homophonic music. "Fugue in G minor" (The Little Fugue in G minor) by Bach (*Adventures in Music*, Grade 6, Volume 1) is an example of polyphonic music.

Activities for Children

Aural Perception

1. (Grades 2–6) Strum a chord on an autoharp. Ask the children if they heard more than one pitch. Give C, E, and G resonator or hand bells to three children and ask them to play them individually and then simultaneously. Share the terms *chord* and *harmony* with the class. Help the children develop definitions of the terms.

2. (Grades 2–6) Have your children sing several familiar songs with a chordal accompaniment. Identify the texture as homophonic.

3. (Grades 2–6) Sing a two- or three-part round, such as "Ghost of Tom" (p. 42), and a song with a descant, such as "This Train" (p. 44). Ask your children to try to identify the ways in which the texture of this music differs from homophonic texture. (In each of the experiences a melody was accompanied by another melody, creating a polyphonic texture.) If children have difficulty perceiving the textural difference, sing one of the songs again, in unison, with an autoharp (chordal) accompaniment. Discuss the texture.

Transfer

1. (Grades 2–6) Play several recorded excerpts exemplifying the two textures. Ask children to identify the texture of each example. "The Swan" from Saint-Saens' *Carnival of the Animals* (*Adventures in Music*, Grade 3, Volume 2) is a good example of homophonic music. The opening of McBride's "Pumpkineater's Little Fugue" (*Adventures in Music*, Grade 2, Volume 2) is a good example of polyphonic music.

2. (Grades 2–6) If strumming instruments are available, allow individual children to create and practice accompaniments for familiar songs. Perform them while the class sings. Ask children to identify the textures (homophonic).

3. (Grades 2–3) Invite children to play bordun accompaniments for "Chatter with the Angels" and "Mary Had a Baby" (pentatonic songs) using the F and C bells or tuned water glasses. Identify the texture (homophonic).

4. (Grades 3–6) Ask children to create short ostinati on melody instruments to accompany familiar pentatonic songs. Identify the texture (polyphonic).

CONCEPT: CHORDS

Once the concepts of homophonic and polyphonic textures are internalized, you can begin to study individual chords.

- Some chords are restless: They create tension and a need to move on. Some chords are stable: They provide relaxation or a release from tension.

Activities for Teachers

1. Experiment with an autoharp. Strum each of the chords and try to hear several that have a more restless quality. Compare your selection with those made by others in your class.

2. In small groups, experiment with two autoharps. On the first autoharp, strum one of the restless chords. On the second autoharp, locate a chord that releases the tension of the restless chord in the most satisfying manner. Share your chord sequence with the class.

3. Separate into groups of three. Each group should have at least one set of bells and one mallet per person. Player 1 picks a bell and taps it lightly over and over. Player 2 taps other bells and selects one that sounds good (doesn't clash) with the first bell. Player 2 taps the chosen bell over and over lightly. Player 3 selects a third bell that doesn't clash with the first two and plays it lightly over and over. Note the names of the three bells you have chosen and share your chord with the class.

4. Plan an autoharp accompaniment for the first section of this spiritual. Use the F and C7 chords in a sequence that sounds good with the melody. Write the names of the chords you select above the staff in each measure. The second section of the song is done for you.

Rock-a My Soul

Oh a-rock-a my soul_ in the bos-om of A - bra-ham A-rock-a my soul_ in the

Fine

bos-om of A - bra-ham. A-rock-a my soul in the bos-om of A - bra-ham. Oh, rock-a my soul.

F   F   C7   C7

So   high,   you can't get   o-ver it;   So   low,   you can't get un-der it,

F   F   F   C7   F   *D. C. al Fine*

So   wide,   you can't get a-round_it. You must   go   in at the   door.

Activities for Children

Aural Perception

1. (Grades 2–6)   Accompany several songs with an autoharp. Emphasize that the instrument is producing chords when it is strummed. Notice that most accompaniments include the use of two or more different chords.

2. (Grades 1–3)   Accompany the singing of "If You're Happy" (p. 231) on the autoharp. Then play the accompaniment by itself, stopping on the C7 chord. Ask the children if they think this is a good stopping place. Explain that some chords are restless and want to move on. Play the accompaniment again and stop on the F chord. Ask the children if this is a good stopping place. Explain that some chords are stable.

Transfer

1. (Grades 1–2)   With the children standing in a circle around you, play chords on the autoharp. Maintain a steady beat. When you strum a restless chord, the children should walk to the steady beat. When you strum a stable chord, the children should stand still.

2. (Grades 4–6)   Remove the C, E, G, B, D, and F bells from a set of resonator bells (or use tuned glasses), and assign each bell to a different child. Ask the children to play the three pitches of the C chord (C-E-G) together. Invite them to play the four pitches of the G7 chord (G-B-D-F). Ask the class which of the chords sounds restless (the G7). Point out that the presence of the fourth pitch (F) creates the restless quality, or tension, of the G7 chord. Use the bell chords to provide an accompaniment for "On a Mountain Stands a Lady" (pp. 232–233).

SUMMARY

Sounding tones at the same time produces harmony. There are two kinds of harmonic textures, homophonic and polyphonic. Homophonic texture occurs when a melody is combined with a chordal accompaniment. Polyphonic texture is produced by accompanying one melody with another (such as a descant, ostinato, or the melody itself). Chords result from sounding three or more pitches simultaneously. Some chords have a stable quality. Other chords have a restless quality. Accompaniments for songs include chords of various qualities arranged in appropriate sequences.

SUGGESTED PROJECTS

1. Compare approaches to at least one harmonic concept found in *Silver Burdett MUSIC, Spectrum of Music,* and *The Music Book.* Comment on the relative qualities of the musical materials and teaching suggestions in each text.

2. Make a cassette tape that includes at least ten musical excerpts, each of which very clearly exemplifies homophonic or polyphonic texture. Prepare an evaluation sheet on which children can identify the texture of each example.

3. Practice playing restless and stable chords on an autoharp or keyboard instrument until you can play them well enough to execute a three-chord sequence (such as C-G7-C) smoothly. Make a cassette tape that includes several three-chord sequences. Some should end on a stable chord and some on a restless chord. Prepare an evaluation sheet on which children can identify the quality of the final chord in each sequence.

NINE

*F*orm in Music

Most of us have an inner need for **form** and order in many aspects of our everyday lives as well as in our artistic creations. Music has form and order. Composers are able to fire our imaginations, intellects, and feelings by the manner in which they arrange their musical ideas. The careful ordering of musical ideas and the extension of these ideas into sections creates a meaningful whole. By skillfully balancing similar and contrasting musical ideas and sections, the composer provides us with the comfort of the familiar and the challenge of the unfamiliar.

It is not difficult to help children perceive the organizational scheme of a composition. Younger children can develop an understanding of repetition and contrast through movement, creative activities, and the use of icons. Older children can create accompaniments that highlight contrasting sections or phrases. Eventually, they can demonstrate their understanding of musical form by creating compositions with specific forms.

The concepts presented in this chapter are arranged in a sequence that begins with patterns of extended musical ideas and progresses to the perception and understanding of small musical ideas in formal structure. The final concept introduces a large form: theme and variation. These concepts are included in current music series books and represent a minimum basic program in form.

Recognition of the organization of music into sections must precede the ability to perceive the elements of repetition and contrast. Therefore, the following activities focus first on development of the ability to perceive sections in music. Later, students classify these sections as similar or different.

CONCEPT: UNITY AND VARIETY

- A musical composition may consist of sections or ideas. These sections can be similar or different.

Composers seek to create compositions that embody the qualities of unity and variety. Since repetition provides unity, these compositions often include sections that are similar or the same. Since contrast provides variety, they also include sections that are different.

Letters are used to indicate the form of a musical composition. One letter is assigned to each section. The letter *A* is used to refer to the first section and all sections that are similar to it. The next several letters of the alphabet are assigned in sequence to contrasting sections, the number of letters depending on how many differing sections there are in the composition. Thus, the form of a musical composition with two differing sections is *AB.* The form of a musical composition in which the A section is repeated at the end is *ABA.*

Activities for Teachers

1. Sing "Hop Up! My Ladies" (p. 27). Decide where the second section begins. Develop a hand jive to accompany each section of the song. Sing the song and perform the hand jive with a partner.

2. Listen to Ralph Vaughan William's *Fantasia on "Greensleeves"* (*Adventures in Music,* Grade 6, Volume 2). How many large sections do you hear? Did you hear repetition? Did you hear a contrasting section?

3. Sing several of the following songs and determine whether the forms are AB or ABA: "The Alphabet" (p. 42), "Sourwood Mountain" (p. 31), "Ezekiel Saw a Wheel" (p. 47), and "Draw a Bucket of Water" (p. 231).

4. Listen to the following instrumental selections and determine the form of each:
   a. Handel, "Bourrée," *Water Music* (*Adventures in Music,* Grade 3, Volume 2)
   b. Tchaikovsky, "Dance of the Reed Flutes" (*Adventures in Music,* Grade 1, Volume 2)

5. Work with a small group to plan and execute different steps for each of the sections in "Hop Up! My Ladies" (p. 27) or "The Cuckoo" (p. 28), both of which are examples of AB form.

6. Improvise a composition with AB or ABA form in a small group using percussion instruments or improvised soundmakers. Perform the composition for your classmates, asking them to identify the form.

Activities for Children

Aural Perception

1. (Grades 2–6) Find a familiar song that has two distinct sections. "Draw a Bucket of Water" (p. 231) is appropriate for lower grades; "Sourwood Mountain" (p. 31) is suitable for upper grades. Develop a contrasting body-sound or percussion accompaniment to highlight each section.

2. (Grades 2–3) Construct a chart using two different designs arranged in AB and ABA patterns.

Have the children sing "On a Mountain Stands a Lady" (pp. 232–233) and "Get on Board" (p. 242). Ask the children to match each song with a design. If desired, introduce the labels *AB* and *ABA*.

3. (Grades 2–6, depending on the chart and the music) Select a recording of an orchestral composition with a clear AB or ABA form. Prepare a visual chart that you can use to guide children through the composition. The following two charts are good examples. The first chart, planned

to accompany the third movement of *Children's Symphony* by Harl McDonald (*Adventures in Music*, Grade 2, Volume 1), is quite simple. The second chart, which follows the rise and fall of the melody of "Dance of the Little Swans" from Tchaikovsky's *Swan Lake* (*Adventures in Music*, Grade 1, Volume 1), is more complex.

Children's Symphony, ABA form

The Farmer in the Dell

Jingle Bells

The Farmer in the Dell

"Dance of the
Little Swans,"
ABA form

Introduction

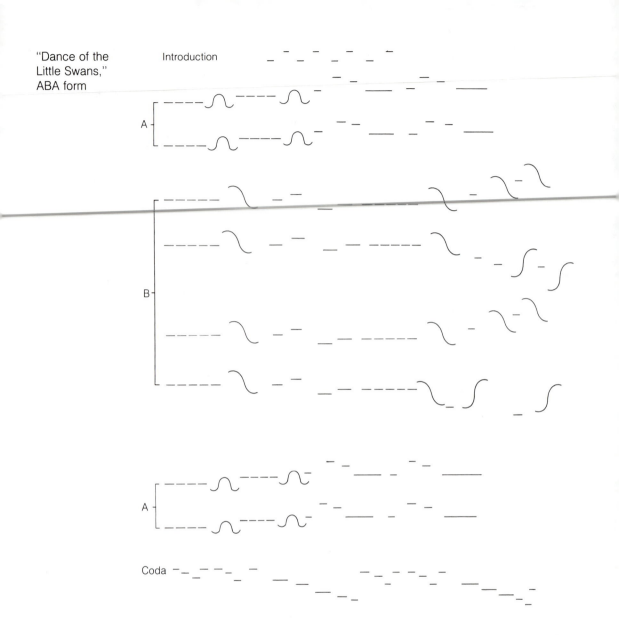

A useful technique for guiding children through the "Dance of the
Little Swans" is to track the melodic movements with a cutout ballerina
or star secured to the end of a pointer.

Transfer

1. (Grades 2–6, depending on the song)   Invent a variation on Activity 1 above with various body movements, such as hand claps, finger snaps, or foot stamps, to highlight each section of a familiar song.

2. (Grades 3–6)   Invite children to improvise a short two-part composition using body or percussion sounds. Direct the group as a whole, or work in small groups.

3. (Grades 1–3)   Invite children to find objects with an AB or ABA design. Here are some examples:

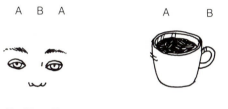

A   B   A

Eye Nose Eye

A   B

Cup   Handle

4. (Grades 1–3)   After children have learned "Bounce Around," help them plan a dance that incorporates different movements for each section. The words of the song may help them choose appropriate movements.

Bounce Around

5. (Grades 2–6)   Compose an instrumental piece using contrasting percussion instruments. If necessary, help younger children create patterns and select instruments. The following two example compositions each involve four groups of children and are arranged in AB form.

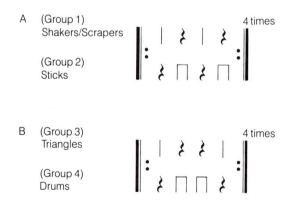

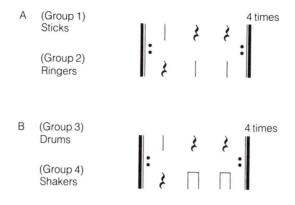

Older children should be able to plan their own rhythmic patterns.

Once you are able to recognize the larger aspects of musical form, you can focus on smaller organizational units. In the next pages, you will examine musical phrases, short but complete musical thoughts.

CONCEPT: PHRASE

- A phrase in music, like a sentence, expresses a complete thought.

Activities for Teachers

1. Sing "Pretty Saro" (p. 244). Study the text and ask these questions: (1) Where does the first thought end? (2) Where do the second, third, and fourth thoughts end? Sing the song again and notice the musical phrases. How do they reflect the structure of the text? Now sing "Pretty Saro" and shape the phrases by moving an arm in a sweeping arc. Try to sing each phrase as smoothly as possible, on one breath.

2. Plan a series of movements that reflect the phrase structure of a song in this text. Teach it to a small group of your classmates and share it with the class.

3. Listen to Brahms' "Hungarian Dance #1" (*Adventures in Music*, Grade 5, Volume 2). Concentrate on the endings of the first four phrases. Ask yourself the following questions:
a. Does the melody move up or down at the end of each phrase?
b. Does the melody end with a long tone or a short tone?
Compare these distinct phrase endings with the endings in the opening of Smetana's "Dance of the Comedians" from *The Bartered Bride* (*Adventures in Music*, Grade 6, Volume 2). Discuss your findings in class.

Activities for Children

Aural Perception

1. (Grades 1–2) Invite your children to sing a familiar song with distinct phrases. As they sing, shape the phrases by moving an arm from one side of your body to the other side in an arc. Invite children to sing the song once more, shaping the phrases with you.

2. (Grades 3–6) Plan an activity similar to Activity 1 under Activities for Teachers.

Transfer

1. (Grades 1–2) Create an accompaniment for "Twinkle, Twinkle" in which children tap lightly on the steady beats using chopsticks or rhythm sticks. Invite one or two children to play a "twinkling" sound at the end of each phrase. Use an instrument that makes a soft ringing sound. (A suspended nail, finger cymbals, or a triangle played lightly would be appropriate.)

Twinkle, Twinkle, Little Star

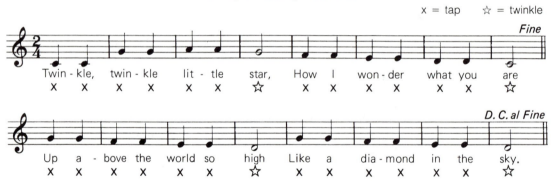

2. (Grades 4–6) Sing a familiar song such as "Somebody's Knocking" (p. 35). Walk the steady beat and change direction at the end of each phrase. Later, invite the children to walk the beat, clap the rhythm patterns, and turn at the end of each phrase.

3. (Grades 3–6) Set up a pentatonic scale on Orff instruments, or instruct children to use the black bars on melody bells. Provide a steady beat on a drum or another nonpitched instrument while you recite the following chant:

Jim, John, Jan, June,
Chant these names, then make a tune.

Next, ask the children with pitched instruments to improvise an eight-beat melodic phrase based on the rhythm pattern created by the words. Vary this activity by asking volunteers to improvise eight-beat solos, alternating their improvisations with group chanting.

CONCEPT: MOTIVES

Many musical compositions contain very short musical ideas. These musical ideas or patterns may be repeated frequently, even within a phrase. The next activities focus on the **motive,** a short rhythmic or melodic idea.

- A short rhythmic or melodic idea is called a motive (mō'tēv). A motive may be repeated several times in a musical composition.

Activities for Teachers

1. Sing "Canoe Song" (p. 123), clapping the rhythm patterns as you sing. Pay particular attention to the syncopated pattern of "My pad-dles." This is the first motive in the song. Sing and clap again, noticing the number of times this motive occurs. Next, sing the song while clapping the motive.

2. Listen to the first movement of Mozart's *Symphony #40 in G Minor* (*Bowmar Orchestral Library*, Volume 71). The violins begin the first phrase with a short three-note motive. This motive is played three times at the beginning of the first phrase. It is played three more times with a different melodic pattern.

As you listen to the movement, notice that this motive is repeated many times.

Activities for Children

Aural Perception

1. (Grades 1–2) Have children sing a familiar song such as "London Bridge" (p. 20) or "Bounce Around" (p. 134). Clap a motive from the song.

London Bridge (excerpt)

fall - ing down

Bounce Around (excerpt)

Bounce a-round

Ask the children to identify the words in the song that match the pattern you clapped. Invite them to clap the motive while they sing it. Ask them to count the number of times they hear the motive as they listen to the song. Lead them to discover that a motive may be repeated several times within a song.

2. (Grades 4–6) Review a familiar song with a distinct motive, such as "Sourwood Mountain" (p. 31). Clap the rhythmic motive:

Hey   de - ing dang   did-dle - al - ley day

Invite children to clap that motive each time they sing it. Lead children to discover that a motive may be repeated several times within a song.

Transfer

1. (Grades 1–2) Invite children to find another short pattern or motive in ''Bounce Around'' (p. 134).

Bounce Around (excerpt)

To - dee - id-dy-um

2. (Grades 2–4) Play a recording of ''The Viennese Musical Clock'' from Kodály's *Háry János Suite* (*Adventures in Music*, Grade 2, Volume 1) for your class. An important motive occurs in the first theme following the short introduction. Clap it for the children and invite them to clap it with you. Record the number of times the motive is heard. Create an iconic representation of the motive:

– – – – – ——

short short short short short l-o-n-g

3. (Grades 5–6) Play a recording of the first movement of Mozart's *Symphony #40 in G Minor* (*Bowmar Orchestral Library*, Volume 71). Help children discover the rhythmic motive that occurs over and over:

♫ | ♩ ♫ ♩ ♫ | ♩ ♩

Ask children to count the number of times they hear this motive in succession at the beginning of the composition (four times).

CONCEPT: VARIATIONS ON A THEME

The final section of this chapter highlights another of the forms frequently found in instrumental music: *theme and variation*. This form provides a good showcase for a composer's ability to create a composition, based on one **theme,** that contains both unity and variety.

- It is possible to create many variations of a musical theme by changing one or more of its elements. The form of a composition consisting of a theme followed by several variations of that theme is traditionally called *theme and variation.*

Activities for Teachers

1. As a class project, make a list of musical elements with which you have become familiar. (The list might include such elements as timbre, pitch, dynamic level, meter, melody, texture, and tempo.) With this list on the board, listen to a recorded composition in theme and variation form, noting the musical elements that are changed in each variation. Discuss what you heard; then listen again to check your perceptions. (A famous orchestral composition in this form is the second movement from Haydn's *Surprise Symphony* [*Bowmar Orchestral Library,* Volume 62].)

2. Learn to play the melody of "When the Saints Go Marching In" on a pitched instrument. Create your own variation of the theme. Here is the song followed by two variations. The meter is changed in the first variation. In the second, notes have been added to the melody, and the rhythm patterns are altered.

When the Saints Go Marching In

Variation 2

Activities for Children

Aural Perception

(Grades 3–6)   Initiate a discussion that centers on ways a person can change from day-to-day (or hour-to-hour) and still be the same person. Relate this discussion to ways in which musical ideas can be changed yet remain recognizable. Play a clear example of variations on a theme for the class, asking the children to try to discover *how* the theme is varied or changed in each section. (Use only one or two variations in the first such lesson.)

Two colorful compositions in which the variations are based on melodies that may be familiar are "Pop! Goes the Weasel" by Lucien Cailliet (*Adventures in Music*, Grade 4, Volume 1) and "Variations on America" by Charles Ives in the arrangement by William Schuman (*Silver Burdett MUSIC*, Grade 1). Lead the class to discover that the name of this form is *theme and variation*.

Transfer

1. (Grades 3–6)   Share other compositions in theme and variation form with your children. After they have listened to the music, ask them to identify the form.

2. (Grades 3–6)   Invite children to experiment with a simple melody they can play (or perhaps sing, if they are confident singers). Encourage them to create one or more variations. Here is the folk song "Skip to My Lou" followed by a variation created by a nine-year-old boy.

Skip to My Lou

U.S.

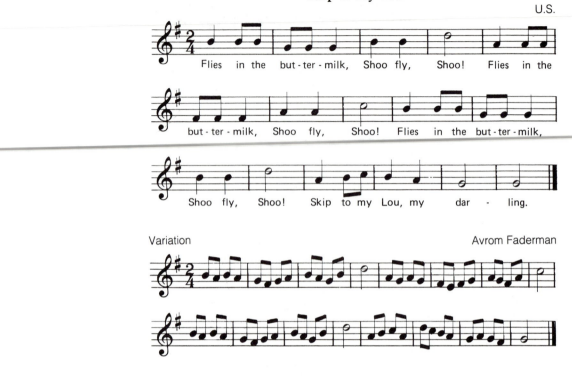

Flies in the but-ter-milk, Shoo fly, Shoo! Flies in the

but-ter-milk, Shoo fly, Shoo! Flies in the but-ter-milk,

Shoo fly, Shoo! Skip to my Lou, my dar - ling.

Variation   Avrom Faderman

There are several other forms in music that are appropriate for the elementary classroom. The classified index at the back of teacher's editions of series texts can guide you to suitable materials.

SUMMARY

Musical ideas are arranged to provide the elements of repetition and contrast to achieve unity and variety. Compositions may consist of sections or ideas that are similar or different. The letters *AB* are used to denote the form of a composition with two contrasting sections, and *ABA* is the name given to the form of a composition in which the A section is repeated at the end. Smaller aspects of compositions are phrases (complete musical thoughts) and motives (short musical ideas that are repeated). Theme and variation is a musical form in which a theme is presented, followed by several variations of the original theme.

SUGGESTED PROJECTS

1. Collect several large pictures, appropriate for classroom use, that incorporate obvious uses of repetition and contrast in their designs.

2. Make a list of ten songs that have two or three clearly defined sections.

3. Make large charts with pictures or designs that represent AB and ABA form.

4. Collect several pictures or pieces of fabric that incorporate motives in the design.

5. Make a list of five songs that contain a distinct repeated motive (rhythmic or melodic).

6. Compare the approaches to theme and variation found in at least two current series texts. Comment on the quality and suitability of the musical materials and suggested activities. Discuss the relative merits of the help provided in the teacher's editions.

PART FOUR

Planning for Teaching

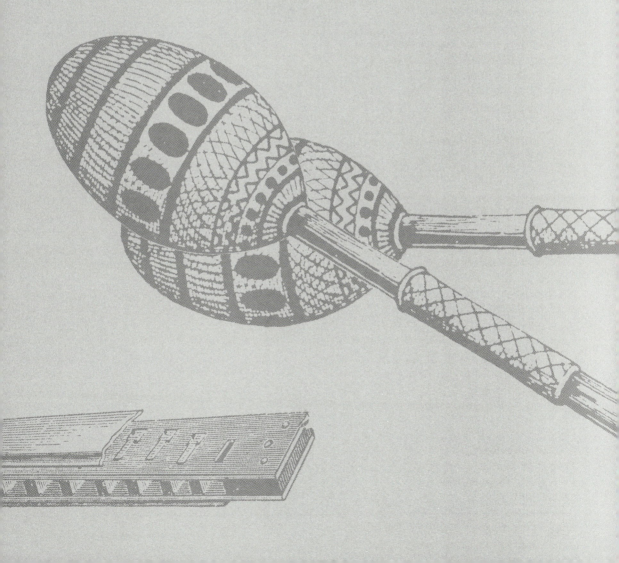

If you have studied the information and performed the activities presented in Chapters One through Nine, you are now comfortable with basic literature, resources, skills, and concepts in music. Part Four will now help you use what you have learned to plan and direct a balanced classroom music program. Chapter Ten describes the development of long-range goals, objectives, and teaching strategies. Chapter Eleven reveals simple step-by-step procedures for use in preparing and teaching individual music lessons.

T E N

The Music Program

"Music is taught and should be taught in the schools primarily because it represents one of the most magnificent manifestations of our cultural heritage, because it brings joy and solace to mankind in the myriad activities of daily life, and because it elevates and exalts the human spirit."[1]

Have you ever played in a marching band, sung in a spring concert, or participated in an all-school musical? These activities are among the well-known outward manifestations of the school music program. The ideal program, however, offers more than a once-a-year concert or a short performance for family and friends. It provides many opportunities to explore and develop an understanding of the elements of music and musical structure.

With careful planning and organization, you can design an ideal music program for your classroom. This chapter will help you develop (1) a philosophy of music education, (2) clearly defined goals and objectives, (3) sequentially organized subject matter and song collections, (4) strategies for teaching the subject matter, and (5) systematic evaluation techniques.

PHILOSOPHY

To maintain an overall sense of unity and purpose, a comprehensive music program must be based on an underlying philosophy of music education. The opening quotation reflects the philosophy of the Music Educators

National Conference. This organization of music educators believes that music has value in the curriculum because it is "one of the most magnificent manifestations of our cultural heritage" and because it brings beauty, joy, and solace to the life of every child. As such, music education makes a unique and important contribution to the aesthetic and cultural objectives of general education.

Many school districts prepare guides that outline the local or statewide philosophy. Districts, however, may vary substantially in their orientation. Though some concur with the philosophy of the Music Educators National Conference, others justify the inclusion of music in the curriculum on the grounds that it improves physical coordination, self-discipline, concentration, teamwork, attitude, or performance in other subject areas. As a classroom teacher, it is your responsibility to become familiar with the local philosophy and to build a program based on it.

GOALS AND OBJECTIVES

A comprehensive music program requires long- and short-term planning and organization. An important part of this planning is a clear statement of educational objectives. Broad objectives, often referred to as *goals*, are the first and most abstract level of objectives. They are the end product toward which all educational effort is directed. The goals of the elementary school program are normally met only by the end of the sixth grade. Thus, goals take years to achieve. The following are examples of goals.

1. to develop the ability to perceive and respond to the expressive qualities of music

2. to acquire understanding of the structure of music

3. to acquire knowledge and understanding of the nature and purpose of music

4. to develop skills necessary for sensitive and intelligent performance and creation of music

The second level of objectives, *instructional* or *program objectives*, describes the end products or behaviors to accomplish in a given instructional unit or course of study. Less abstract than goals, program objectives can be met in a month, a semester, or a school year. The following are examples of program objectives.

Harmony

1. to play and create chordal accompaniments

2. to play and sing descants as harmonizing parts

Form

to recognize repetition and contrast in selected compositions

Melody

1. to match pitches
2. to identify aurally upward and downward melodic movement

The third level of objectives, *behavioral* or *lesson objectives,* describes the end products or behaviors to accomplish in a music lesson. Stated behaviorally, lesson objectives include (1) the knowledge or skill to be gained, (2) the way in which the student will demonstrate that the learning has taken place, and (3) the minimum proficiency required. The following paragraph is an example of a lesson objective.

> Students will demonstrate their ability to identify aurally upward and downward melodic movement in "Charlie over the Ocean" by raising their hands when the melody rises and lowering their hands when the melody falls. The response will be correct for three out of four phrases.

In this example, the lesson objective states the knowledge to be gained (identify aurally upward and downward melodic movement), the way in which the student will demonstrate that the learning has taken place (raise hands when melody rises and lower hands when melody falls), and the minimum proficiency required (correct response in three out of four phrases). Objectives written in this manner require students to demonstrate through observable behavior that they have achieved a given objective.

There are several advantages to developing and using each of the three levels of planning. Realistic and clearly stated objectives give direction and purpose to musical instruction and reliable criteria with which to evaluate students' progress through the school year. Furthermore, well-conceived objectives are an invaluable aid in the selection and use of appropriate songs and activities.

SUBJECT MATTER

Before you can write realistic goals and objectives for your music class, you must be familiar with the subject matter. The subject matter of music is organized broadly into five concept areas: sound, rhythm, melody, harmony, and form. These concept areas are included in most music series texts, are described in Chapters Five through Nine of this book, and are reviewed below.

Sound

There are many sounds around us. Sounds may be described with words such as loud, soft, high, low, short, and long. Different sound sources produce sounds with distinct characteristics or tone color. A sound can tell us something. Sounds are expressive. Sounds can enhance the mood of a poem or story. Each kind of musical instrument produces a sound with a unique tone color or *timbre*.

Rhythm

Some music has a steady beat. Some music has no beat. Beats can move at different rates of speed. Steady beats can be grouped in twos or threes. Some sounds are short. Some sounds are long. Rhythm patterns consist of groups or patterns of long and short sounds. Some rhythm patterns contain silences (rests). Beat, meter, and rhythm patterns combine to form the rhythmic element in music. An accent or stress on a beat or a part of a beat not usually stressed creates a rhythmic effect referred to as *syncopation*.

Melody

Melodies can move up, move down, or stay on the same level. Melodies can move by skips or steps. Melodies move away from and return to a home tone. Pitches can be arranged in sequences referred to as *scales*.

Harmony

Some harmonic textures are homophonic; some are polyphonic. Some chords create tension; some provide relaxation or a release from tension.

Form

A composition may consist of sections or ideas. These sections can be similar or different. A phrase expresses a thought. Short rhythmic or melodic patterns, called motives, express ideas. Motives may be repeated several times in a musical composition.

As you glance through music series texts, you will see lessons that focus on these five concepts. Though the wording may be a little different, the basic concepts are the same. When you plan your own music program, you will begin by selecting one or more of these concepts.

SONG COLLECTION

An important part of planning for teaching includes the collection and organization of songs and activities. Before the school year begins, check with the school librarian or the principal and find out which, if any, music series is available for your classroom. You may find music books tucked away in boxes, on shelves in storerooms, or stored in district audiovisual services. If possible, obtain the books and place them in a visible, easily accessible part of your classroom.

At your earliest convenience, pick up the teacher's edition of each book you are using and study the table of contents, the teacher's guide, and the indexes in the back of the book. Observe how the songs and activities are organized. Which concepts and skills are emphasized? Are recordings available? Which musical activities will enrich other areas of the school curriculum? Could you use the recordings, songs, games, or dances in conjunction with a social studies unit or a school program?

Listen to the recordings and read through the teacher's guides. Spend as much time as possible familiarizing yourself with the songs and activities. Once you feel comfortable with the music, organize the songs and activities in a way that will be useful to you as a teacher. An organized, up-to-date, and accessible music collection will save frustration and valuable teaching and preparation time.

Organization by Concept

One practical method of organization involves analyzing and sorting music by concept. Most songs provide a clear example of at least one concept. Some may be used to illustrate several concepts. If you have selected songs from a series music book, the teacher's guide will usually suggest the concept or concepts that can be developed through each activity. Several current music series, including those published by Silver Burdett and Macmillan, use conceptual development as a means of organization.

If you are using sources other than music series, you will need to make more thorough preparation. The following questions are designed to help you identify concepts. Consider the questions as you select a song or composition, and make notes of your findings on (or with) the music manuscript.

Song Analysis

Sound

Does this song or recording allow easy identification of
a. high and low

b. loud and soft

c. sounds with distinct characteristics or tone color

d. voices (e.g., male, female, child, ensemble)

e. instruments (e.g., string, percussion, wind)

Rhythm

1. Beat: Is this a good song for stepping, clapping, or tapping the beat?

2. Tempo: Is this a good activity to illustrate changes in tempo?

3. Meter: Does the music move in twos, threes, or both?

4. Rhythm patterns: How many different rhythm patterns are in this song? Are any of these patterns repeated? (See p. 86.)

Melody

1. Does this song contain clear examples of upward or downward melodic movement? Does the melody move mostly by steps, skips, or repeated tones?

2. Does the melody have a home tone?

3. What scale is associated with this melody?

Harmony

1. Homophonic: Is the accompaniment chordal? Can the students or teacher play an accompaniment on the autoharp, guitar, or ukulele?

2. Polyphonic: Can this song be sung as a round? Does the harmony consist of two or more independent melodies heard at the same time?

Form

1. Does this song or composition have recognizable sections? Are these sections similar or different?

2. Does this song or composition have a clear phrase structure? Are phrases similar or different?

3. Does this music contain repeated melodic or rhythmic ideas or patterns (motives)?

Some teachers use colors or symbols to call attention to selected phrases or sections of a music manuscript. The following songs are part of a song collection organized by concept. Note the way in which concepts are highlighted. Do you see additional concepts that could be explored through these songs?

Hot Cross Buns

Concepts

Rhythm   Rhythm patterns consist of groups or patterns of long and short sounds. Some rhythm patterns contain silences (rests).

Melody   Melodies can move up, move down, or stay on the same level.

Rose, Rose

Concepts

Melody   Melodies can move by steps, skips, or repeated tones.

Harmony   A homophonic texture occurs when a melody is combined with a chordal accompaniment. A polyphonic texture occurs when two or more independent melodies are combined.

When you have selected songs and activities and identified appropriate concepts, you are ready to plan long-range teaching strategies.

LONG-RANGE PLANNING

Early in the school year, Ms. Johnson enthusiastically introduced the song "Charlie over the Ocean" to her first-grade class. When the children could sing the song accurately, the teacher presented two bells and explained that one had a high sound and the other a low sound. She played each bell for the class and then carefully put the instruments away in a cupboard.

The next day, the class reviewed "Charlie over the Ocean" and played a chase game. When the children returned to their seats, Ms. Johnson played the first two pitches of the song on the piano and asked, "Which sound is higher?" To her surprise, she was greeted with an enthusiastic show of hands and an unexpected variety of guesses.

Frustrated, Ms. Johnson asked the class, "What do I mean when I say this sound is high or this sound is low?" At this point, a bright youngster, who had frequently been told to turn the T.V. set "down low," loudly and confidently responded, "Low is soft!"

Situations such as this are avoidable. Though Ms. Johnson knew the subject matter well, she had not established plans and procedures for teaching the concept *a sound can be high or low.*

A strategy is a long-range plan designed to help children perceive, accommodate, and transfer concepts in music (see p. 76). In its written form, a strategy is an outline or framework consisting of a concept, program objectives, and a list of appropriate songs and activities. The songs and activities are arranged in four stages or groups: (1) prepare, (2) label, (3) transfer, and (4) evaluate. These stages may overlap. It is helpful, however, to explain and describe these stages as if they were four separate units.

Prepare

The songs and activities in the preparation stage provide a concrete foundation for conceptualization. In this stage, children clap, tap, sing, move, play, and acquire hands-on experience with the new learning. Physical movement and active participation are encouraged.

To learn sound concepts, children tap objects and compare sounds. As preparation for beat, they may follow the leader and pretend to be clocks or turn signals. As preparation for rhythm patterns, they are given many opportunities to clap "the way the words go."

154   *Planning for Teaching*

Where appropriate, children can manipulate and experiment with pictorial representations of the concept. They can match pictorial designs with a familiar song. As preparation for a melodic concept, they can use pictures to represent the rise and fall of a melody. Compare the following illustration with the first phrase of "Hot Cross Buns" (p. 153).

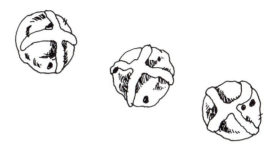

In the preparation stage, children learn songs and activities by rote. They do not read or discuss the musical notation or use the symbols associated with the concept. Rather, through guided participation, they gain the experiences that will prepare them for the introduction of appropriate symbols and terminology.

Label

In the labeling stage, experiences are associated with musical symbols and terminology. This stage usually requires only a few minutes of class time. As an example, if children have sung several melodies with chordal accompaniment, the labeling stage consists of introducing the term *homophonic*. If children have sung several rounds and descants, the labeling stage consists of introducing the term *polyphonic*. In a matter of minutes, experiences gained in the preparation stage are associated with the terms *homophonic* and *polyphonic*. If preparation has been adequate, association is established quickly and easily.

Transfer

In the transferring stage, children use the newly introduced symbols and terminology as a way of thinking about and referring to their experiences. Typically, the teacher reviews the activities and songs that were introduced in the preparation stage. Children locate and identify the new learning and use and apply the correct labels. In addition, children are given the opportunity to apply the labels in new and unfamiliar situations.

The new learning can be transferred, or reinforced, in many different ways. As reinforcement for harmonic concepts, children can be asked to categorize examples of harmony as polyphonic or homophonic. They can be asked to create a polyphonic or homophonic accompaniment for a familiar song. As reinforcement for meter, children can identify examples of music as duple or triple meter. They can create percussion accompaniments for songs in duple or triple meter. (See activities presented in Chapters Five through Nine for other ideas.)

Depending on the concept, the preparation and transfer stages may be long or short. The required number of songs and activities depends on the concept and on the individual class. Above all, children need many concrete experiences before they are able to establish the relationships that enable them to conceptualize. It is imperative that children receive ample preparation and that labels be introduced and applied.

Evaluate

The fourth part of a good teaching strategy, and a vital part of any music program, is evaluation. Evaluation enables the teacher to plan appropriate lessons, to determine if objectives have been met, and to assess progress toward the long-range goals. Three forms of evaluation are useful in planning and teaching: (1) diagnostic, (2) formative, and (3) summative.[2]

In *diagnostic evaluation*, the teacher gathers data that reveal the child's present knowledge or skill. Through careful observation and questioning, the teacher diagnoses the strengths and weaknesses of each child. The information is helpful in selecting and writing program objectives.

Formative evaluation measures the day-to-day, lesson-to-lesson growth and development of a child. Unlike diagnostic evaluation, formative evaluation is employed throughout every lesson on a continuous basis. In music, this process is often accomplished informally by careful listening and observation.

Summative evaluation is the comprehensive evaluation at the end of a course or unit of study. The most common example of summative evaluation is the final exam. This form of evaluation enables the teacher to determine if program objectives have been met.

Summative evaluation, used frequently in the evaluation stage of a teaching strategy, can be accomplished by informal observation or by more formal testing procedures. Some teachers use a song or portion of a song as the exam. For example, the teacher plays or sings a song for the class and asks students to indicate the melodic direction with their hands.

This evaluation can also be accomplished by a written test. Aural recognition of upward and downward melodic movement can be measured by asking children to listen to musical phrases and circle the correct responses (upward or downward) on an exam paper. Visual recognition of upward and downward melodic movement can be tested by asking children to observe examples of music notation and circle the correct responses (upward or downward) on an exam paper.

Remember, you must measure or test the accomplishment of every program objective. If any objective is not met, transfer activities should be reviewed and student progress tested again at a later date.

DESIGNING TEACHING STRATEGIES

Current series books provide lists of concepts, goals, and objectives that will help you as you design teaching strategies. Some series books include songs, activities, and teaching suggestions organized in units. Each unit represents, in effect, a *mini* teaching strategy. *Silver Burdett MUSIC,* for example, is organized in modules. The module on meter in Grade Three includes goals and objectives, songs, games, movement activities, and recordings for use in teaching the concept *steady beats can be grouped in twos or threes.* Throughout the module, the authors refer to music from other units that can be used in planning additional or alternate activities.

You may fear that your students will not be ready to perform the activities suggested in series textbooks. Do not worry. Most series books assume a varied background of music experience. *Silver Burdett MUSIC,* for example, specifically states that though it takes the child into "progressively deeper experiences with music . . . it allows a newcomer to the program to begin at any point and be drawn into the spiral from that point on."[3]

If you wish to design your own strategies, begin by selecting one or two concepts from each concept area. Depending on the background of your students and the length and frequency of music lessons, select program objectives and assemble an appropriate group of songs and activities.

The careful selection of songs and activities is one of the keys to successful strategy design. The music should be varied and interesting and should provide many opportunities for active participation. Some music is selected primarily because of its inherent beauty and usefulness for teaching purposes. Other songs are chosen because they are your favorites. Whatever the reason for selection, each song or activity should lead the class closer to the achievement of objectives.

How many songs and activities should be collected for each strategy? Six? Thirty? The answer to this question depends on the concept itself, the depth of the experience, the time involved, and the class. Every class is different, and every teacher explores concepts in different ways. As a rule of thumb, new teachers might begin by collecting a minimum of eight songs and activities for each strategy. Daily evaluation will reveal any need for addition or deletion.

At first, the collection of music for a given set of strategies may seem like an enormous task. Furthermore, teaching several concepts in a given period of time may seem impossible. Don't despair! Your song collection will grow rapidly. Ideally, each song or recording will be used to prepare several musical concepts. If you have planned well, the music will also enhance learning in other areas of the curriculum and can even become part of a school or class program.

The following is a sample teaching strategy designed for use in a second-grade classroom. Look through the written portion and study the song excerpts. Which songs are used in more than one part of the strategy? Why? Which songs include clear examples of upward melodic movement? Downward?

Sample Strategy

Grade Level: Two

Concept: A melody can move up, move down, or stay on the same level.

Program Objectives: (nine-week unit)

1. to identify aurally melodies that move up, move down, or stay on the same level

2. to identify visually melodies that move up, move down, or stay on the same level

Prepare:

Same Level
Old MacDonald
Scotland's Burning

Downward and Same Level
Hot Cross Buns
Go Tell Aunt Rhody
Chicken Ma Craney Crow

Upward and Same Level
Are You Sleeping
Draw a Bucket of Water

Same, Downward, and Upward
John Kanaka
Old MacDonald
Hey Betty Martin
Jolly Old Saint Nicholas

Label:

Scotland's Burning (same level)

Hot Cross Buns (downward)

Are You Sleeping (upward)

Transfer: All songs listed above plus the following.

On a Mountain Stands a Lady
Long Legged Sailor
This Old Man

Evaluate (summative evaluation):

Charlie over the Ocean

Songs:

Same level:

Old MacDonald (excerpt)

Here a chick, there a chick, ev - 'ry-where a chick chick,

Scotland's Burning (excerpt)

Fire, Fire, Fire, Fire

Downward and same level:

Hot Cross Buns (excerpt)

Hot cross buns, Hot cross buns,

Go Tell Aunt Rhody (excerpt)

Go tell Aunt Rho - dy,

Chicken Ma Craney Crow (excerpt)

Chick - en ma chick -en my cra - ney crow,

Upward and same level:

Are You Sleeping (excerpt)

Broth - er John, Broth - er John?

Draw a Bucket of Water (excerpt)

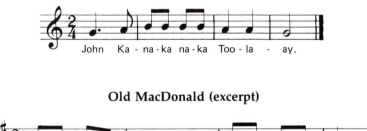

Now num - ber one pop un - der!

Same level, upward, and downward:

John Kanaka (excerpt)

John Ka - na - ka na - ka Too - la - ay.

Old MacDonald (excerpt)

Old Mac-Don - ald had a farm, Ee - yi - ee - yi oh.

Hey Betty Martin (excerpt)

Hey, Bet-ty Mar-tin, tip-py toe, tip-py toe, Hey, Bet-ty Mar-tin, tip-toe fine.

Jolly Old Saint Nicholas (excerpt)

Jol-ly old Saint Nich-o-las, Lean your ear this way;

On a Mountain Stands a Lady (excerpt)

On a moun-tain stands a la-dy, Who she is I do not know,

Long Legged Sailor

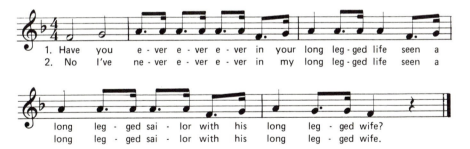

1. Have you e-ver e-ver e-ver in your long leg-ged life seen a
2. No I've ne-ver e-ver e-ver in my long leg-ged life seen a

long leg-ged sai-lor with his long leg-ged wife?
long leg-ged sai-lor with his long leg-ged wife.

This Old Man

Words under music: This old man, he played one. He played nick-nack on my thumb, With a nick-nack pad-dy-wack, give a dog a bone, This old man came roll-ing home.

Charlie over the Ocean

Words under music:

Solo: Char-lie o-ver the o - cean, Group: Char-lie o-ver the o - cean,

Solo: Char-lie o-ver the sea. Group: Char-lie o-ver the sea.

Solo: Char-lie caught a big fish, Group: Char-lie caught a big fish,

Solo: Can't catch me. Group: Can't catch me.

A teaching strategy includes a concept, program objectives, and a list of songs and activities. It is a long-range teaching plan. Chapter Eleven will show you how to plan brief, carefully structured music lessons and how to integrate these mini-lessons into the school day.

SUMMARY

A focused and comprehensive music program involves long- and short-term planning and organization. This preparation includes the development of a well-defined philosophy of music education, a clear statement of educational objectives, and sequentially organized subject matter and teaching strategies.

Goals, or broad objectives, represent the end product toward which all educational effort is directed. Program objectives describe the end products or behaviors to be accomplished in a given instructional unit or course of study. Lesson objectives describe the desired end products or behaviors to be accomplished in a music lesson.

Strategies are long-range plans designed to help children perceive, accommodate, and transfer concepts. Successful strategies include four basic stages: prepare, label, transfer, and evaluate. The preparation stage provides a concrete foundation for conceptualization. The labeling stage introduces the symbols and appropriate terminology. The transferring stage includes many opportunities to use and apply the labels. The evaluation stage enables teachers to determine if program objectives have been met.

One of the keys to successful strategy design is the collection and organization of songs and activities. One practical approach organizes music by concepts selected from the sound, form, harmony, rhythm, and melody concept areas.

Several current series books include materials organized in *mini* teaching strategies. The units include goals and objectives, songs, games, movement, and recordings for use in teaching concepts.

NOTES

1. MENC National Committee on Instruction, "Position Paper: The Role of Music in the Total Development of the Child," *Music Educators Journal*, Vol. 63 (April 1977), p. 59.

2. See also Vernice Trousdale Nye, *Music for Young Children*, 3d ed. (Dubuque, Iowa: Wm. C. Brown, 1983), p. 78.

3. Elizabeth Crook, Bennett Reimer, and David S. Walker, *Silver Burdett MUSIC* (Palo Alto, Calif.: Silver Burdett Company, 1981), p. vi.

SUGGESTED PROJECTS

1. Scan the introductory pages of current music series books, fine arts frameworks, or district curriculum guides. Compare the philosophies expressed in these publications. Write a brief statement summarizing your own philosophy of music education.

2. Locate a series book organized in units by concept. Select a unit and identify the concept, program objectives, suggested songs and activities, and evaluation techniques. Discuss the strengths and weaknesses of the teaching strategy.

3. Select ten to fifteen songs suitable for a grade level of your choice. Using the questions on page 151 as a guide, identify appropriate concepts for each song. Use colored pens or symbols to highlight melodic direction or movement, rhythm patterns, and form. Devise a filing system or organize the songs in a notebook for future use.

ELEVEN

*T*he Music Lesson

"Thank you for teaching me songs and things. You brang my life into music. I love you." (Tina Schumacher, second-grade student)

Have you ever watched a group of young carolers as they entertained shoppers on a crisp winter evening? Have you stopped to observe children singing and jumping rope on a noisy playground or a deserted street? The enthusiasm and joy manifested on these occasions is the natural result of a shared musical experience. You, the classroom teacher, can provide similar experiences for your own students.

This chapter will show you how to plan brief, carefully structured music lessons and how to integrate these mini-lessons into the school day. This chapter will first focus on the *design* of a mini-lesson: objectives, materials, procedure, motivation, closure, evaluation, teaching a song or singing game, and introducing or reinforcing a concept. The second part of the chapter will cover the *teaching experience:* classroom preparation, enthusiasm, presence, variety, discipline, and self- and peer-evaluation.

You may not be a concert pianist. Your background may include little or no musical experience. Still, it is possible for you to teach music effectively. This chapter provides you with the knowledge, skills, and confidence you need to achieve immediate success.

DESIGNING THE LESSON

Just as there are dozens of recipes for carrot cake, so are there dozens of ways to teach a music lesson. Just as each cook has a unique approach to the creation of nutritious dishes, so does every teacher have a unique way of introducing a song or reinforcing a concept. Still, every successful music lesson has certain basic components or parts. The following format is designed to assist you in planning a brief, well-structured music lesson (a mini-lesson).

Mini-Lesson Format

Grade Level:

Concept:

Lesson Objectives:

Materials and Room Preparation:

Procedure:

   1. motivation
   2. step-by-step sequence

Closure:

Evaluation Technique:

Grade Level

Writing the grade level at the top of the lesson plan may seem unnecessary. However, it is important to keep a grade level in mind as you plan a lesson. The teacher's approach and the music material may differ depending on the age, interests, and developmental level of the students involved (see pp. 8–11).

Concept

A good teacher is always preparing, labeling, or reinforcing one or more concepts in every lesson (see Chapter Ten). Though it may not be apparent to the students, the teacher may be using a singing game to prepare or reinforce the steady beat, duple meter, ABA form, or rising melodic movement. You will make efficient use of your teaching time if you list concepts on the lesson plan and keep them in mind as you prepare your lesson.

Lesson Objectives

The importance and usefulness of clearly stated lesson objectives cannot be overestimated. The process of thinking through and writing out behavioral lesson objectives forces you, the teacher, to (1) itemize the skills or knowledge to be acquired or refined during the course of a lesson and (2) find a way to observe and record student progress toward stated objectives.

As you will recall from Chapter Ten, behavioral objectives include (1) the knowledge or skill to be gained, (2) the way in which the student will demonstrate that learning has taken place, and (3) the minimum proficiency required. Before you attempt to write a lesson objective, ask yourself: "What do I want my students to be able to do by the end of the lesson?" You may want them to be able to clap the rhythm of a song, chant the words of a poem, write a specific rhythm pattern, sing a song, or tap the beat. You must decide which knowledge or skill to teach. Behavioral objectives must state, in clear terms, what your students will be able to do by the end of the lesson.

The choice of verb is crucial. Study the following list. The action implied by each verb will reveal student progress visibly and/or audibly.

snap	write	hop
clap	draw	step
sing	move	march
chant	perform	skip
recite	tap	gallop

The use of these or similar action verbs facilitates the writing of behavioral objectives. Study the following examples:

Students will clap the rhythm of "John Kanaka."

Students will sing "John Kanaka."

Students will step the beat while singing "Charlie over the Ocean."

Students will tap the ostinato ♩ ♩ ♩ 𝄾 while singing "Hot Cross Buns."

In each example, students will demonstrate their skill, understanding, or knowledge through observable behavior.

Another way to write objectives is to use key phrases:

Students will *demonstrate their understanding* of ABA form *by* standing during the A section and sitting during the B section.

Students will *demonstrate their ability to* recognize aurally upward and downward melodic movement in "Charlie over the Ocean" *by* raising their hands when the melody rises and lowering their hands when the melody falls.

Students will *distinguish between* beat and rhythm *by* stepping the beat during the first verse of "Miss Lucy" and clapping the rhythm during the second verse.

In each example above, students are required to demonstrate their understanding through observable behavior. The word *by* is a critical part of each statement.

The third part of a behavioral objective requires the teacher to specify the minimum degree of proficiency to be attained by the end of the lesson. This can be done in a variety of ways. You may expect your students to meet an objective with 100 percent accuracy, you may expect a certain percentage of your class to meet an objective, or you may specify the minimum number of correct responses by any given class member. Study the following examples:

Students will clap the rhythm of "John Kanaka" *accurately.*

Students will sing "John Kanaka" *accurately.*

Students will demonstrate their ability to recognize aurally upward and downward melodic movement in "Charlie over the Ocean" by independently raising their hands when the melody rises and lowering their hands when the melody falls. *The response will be correct for three out of four phrases.*

Students will tap the ostinato ♩ ♩ ♩ ♪ while singing "Hot Cross Buns." *Ninety-five percent of the class will sing and tap accurately.*

Materials

This portion of the lesson plan includes a list of all materials required to teach the lesson. It is helpful to visualize the room in which you will be teaching. Imagine yourself teaching the lesson and then record every item that you use. Depending on the lesson, you may need:

recording equipment	music books	pitch pipe
overhead projector	(number of copies?)	piano
screen	charts	guitar
record player	pictures	wind instruments
blackboard	masking tape	percussion
records	paper	Orff instruments
cassettes	pencils	

Be sure to include all necessary items. Check to see that equipment is operative.

Procedure

The procedure is the step-by-step course of action—the lesson itself. The course of action must be planned carefully because it is this logical, step-by-step sequence that enables students to meet lesson objectives in the most efficient and enjoyable manner.

The part of the procedure that provides the initial impulse or incentive to learn is the *motivation*. An interesting motivation will stimulate or entice children to listen, to focus their attention, to contribute, and to become actively involved.

There are many ways to motivate a group of children. If you need ideas, consider the objectives you have for the lesson and the concepts involved. Study the selected music, the words of the song, and the structure. Get acquainted with the composer's life and the origin of the music. Look into the lifestyle or historical period in which the music was composed or performed. Results of this research should spark several ideas. Select a motivation that leads directly and smoothly into the lesson and the ultimate accomplishment of objectives.

Examine the following text:

Canoe Song
My paddle's keen and bright,
  Flashing with silver,
Follow the wild goose flight,
  Dip, dip, and swing.

In planning a lesson that introduces this song (see p. 123), the teacher could capture the interest of children by *class discussion*. Questions such as Who has traveled in a canoe?, Where did you go?, and Who can show us how to paddle a canoe? would be appropriate.

Another teacher might motivate students initially by a *challenge*. This teacher would ask students to listen as the song is sung and use the words as clues to determine the type of transportation referred to in the lyrics.

A third teacher might introduce large, colorful pictures of canoes, rivers, and moonlight shining on the water. A fourth teacher might find a canoe paddle for the students to see and touch.

Younger children respond well to the use of colorful pictures, stuffed animals, and storytelling. Older children enjoy startling or challenging questions or revelations. All children are motivated by musical instruments and objects that can be manipulated in some way. Whether you choose discussion, challenge, visual aids, unfamiliar objects, or some other approach, the time you spend planning motivation will be well rewarded.

Preparing a Rote Song Lesson

One of your first assignments will be to teach a song by rote (see p. 38). This should be an enjoyable experience for you and your students. Your success in this venture, however, will depend largely on (1) your choice of song, (2) the degree to which you are comfortable with the song, and (3) the development of a logical, step-by-step teaching procedure.

First, well in advance of your initial music teaching experience, select a song that is suitable for rote learning. Be sure it is one that you personally like and enjoy. This is the first and most important step because through the course of preparation and teaching you will practice and sing this song many times. If you like the song, this will be a pleasant experience, and your students will reflect your energy and enthusiasm.

Second, learn your song well. It is impossible to teach a song you do not know yourself. Furthermore, a group of eager, inexperienced children can easily become confused if you are not *very* sure of the words and melody. Practice your song until you can sing it without error. Practice starting at the beginning of each phrase in the song. When you can recite the words without hesitation, sing the song through without error, and begin on the first note of any phrase, you are ready to teach the song.

Third, determine the most appropriate method, whole song or phrase-by-phrase, for teaching your song. Why is the following song best taught through the phrase-by-phrase approach?

Charlie over the Ocean

Children's game song

Formation   Single circle, facing inward. The leader, Charlie, is outside of the circle.

Action   Charlie sings the solo parts and steps the beat around the circle. Group echoes. When the last note is sung, Charlie tags the nearest child and a chase ensues around the circle. The first child back to the unoccupied space remains in the circle. Game begins again with a new Charlie.

When you have selected a suitable rote method, design and write out a step-by-step procedure for teaching your song. Include the questions you will ask and, where applicable, the response you expect from the children. If you are teaching the song phrase by phrase, indicate the division into phrases and the order in which you will teach them. If you are using the whole-song approach, list the ways in which your class will be given opportunities to hear the whole song sung correctly. Detail the ways in which you will gradually lead your students toward mastery of the entire song.

In the following procedure for teaching "Charlie over the Ocean," the teacher leads second-grade students to memorize the song and gradually assume the leader part.

Motivation: "We all know a special person named Charlie. He is sitting in our classroom right now. This song is about another person named Charlie. Listen as I sing, and raise your hand if you can tell the class what happens to Charlie in this song."

Sing the song and elicit the class response. Continue the discussion with additional questions: "Where do you go to catch fish?", "Do you think Charlie can catch me?"

Sequence:

1. "Let's sing the song together. Be my echo!"
2. Sing the song slowly, phrase by phrase.
      Charlie over the ocean, (class repeat)
      Charlie over the sea, (class repeat)

Charlie caught a big fish, (class repeat)

Can't catch me. (class repeat)

3. Repeat step 2, increasing the tempo and listening carefully as the class responds. Repeat troublesome phrases as necessary.

4. Place four cards on the blackboard. Place the cards vertically, out of sequence.

Charlie over the sea,

Charlie over the ocean,

~~Can't catch me.~~

Charlie caught a big fish,

5. Ask volunteers to arrange the cards in the correct order.

6. Challenge the class to sing the teacher's, or leader's, part. Teacher echo.

7. Ask the class to look carefully at the first phrase and memorize it. Remove the card.

8. Sing entire song, with the class as leader.

9. Repeat steps 7 and 8 with the remaining cards until all cards are removed from the board.

10. Divide the class into two groups and allow one group to lead and one group to echo.

Closure

This section of the lesson plan provides space to record the way in which you will end your lesson. The closure is an important part of the lesson plan. An apologetic or inconclusive ending will weaken an otherwise successful procedure. A strong, confident closure will increase student satisfaction and interest in future lessons.

Be sure to think through and write out your closure. Many teachers use a few well-chosen questions to help the class review key points in the lesson. They conclude by mentioning an exciting event that will occur in a future music lesson. Others "tie back" to the opening by asking the class to answer a challenging question or perform a difficult task presented earlier in the lesson as motivation. You will find examples of closures in the sample lesson plans. Whatever approach you choose, your students should feel that they do not want to miss the next lesson.

Evaluation Technique

One of the most important habits to assume early in your teaching career is that of careful listening and observing. Inexperienced teachers often forget or neglect to observe their students as they sing or play. It is easy to sing with the class and never notice that the students cannot sing the song without your help. It is easy to observe one student performing a task and erroneously assume that the entire class can do as well. Remember, you must test or measure the accomplishment of each lesson objective. Therefore, this section of the lesson plan serves as a reminder of the ways in which you will listen, observe, and record progress toward stated objectives.

Sample Rote Song Mini-Lessons

You are now familiar with the basic parts of a rote song mini-lesson. Before you design your own lessons, however, examine the following sample plans. Ask:

What materials are required to teach these lessons?

How are the students motivated to become involved?

How do procedures lead students toward accomplishment of objectives?

How will students demonstrate their skill, understanding, or knowledge?

Is the closure strong and confident?

How could these lessons be improved?

Mini-Lesson 1

Canoe Song

My pad - dle's keen and bright, Flash - ing with sil - ver,

Fol - low the wild goose flight, Dip dip and swing!

Grade Level: Five

Concept: Prepare: Some harmonic textures are homophonic. Some harmonic textures are polyphonic.

Objective: Students will sing "Canoe Song" accurately.

Materials and Room Preparation:

1. autoharp
2. canoe paddle
3. copy of "Canoe Song"

Procedure:

1. Motivation
   Challenge students to determine the mode of transportation referred to in the song. Explain that you are unable to reveal the title as it contains the answer. Sing the song for the class. Elicit response. Show the canoe paddle to the class. Invite discussion about canoe trips, the effect of moonlight on the water, techniques of paddling a canoe.

2. Sequence (phrase-by-phrase approach)
   a. "Let's sing the song together. Be my echo." Sing the song slowly, phrase by phrase, with autoharp accompaniment.

   > My paddle's keen and bright, (class echo)
   > Flashing with silver, (class echo)
   > Follow the wild goose flight, (class echo)
   > Dip, dip, and swing. (class echo)

   b. Listen and repeat phrases as necessary.
   c. Sing phrases in groups of two. Invite the class to echo.
   d. Sing the first verse with the class.
   e. Challenge the class to sing "Canoe Song" without the teacher.

Closure: "In our next lesson, we will create harmony. We will divide into two groups and sing 'Canoe Song' as a round. Some of you will have a chance to play the autoharp."

Evaluation Technique: Formative evaluation: Listen and observe as the children sing the song. Are the children able to sing "Canoe Song" accurately as a group?

Long Legged Sailor

Children's game song

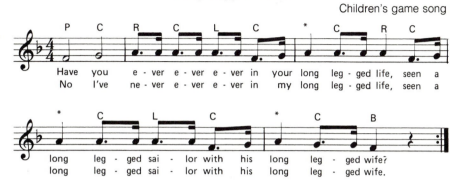

Have you e - ver e - ver e - ver in your long leg - ged life, seen a
No I've ne - ver e - ver e - ver in my long leg - ged life, seen a

long leg - ged sai - lor with his long leg - ged wife?
long leg - ged sai - lor with his long leg - ged wife.

Formation   Partners face each other.

Action   Perform the following motions as indicated above the music:
P—pat hands rapidly on thighs
C—clap own hands
R—clap right hands with partner
L—clap left hands with partner
B—clap both hands across with partner
*—spread hands apart at chest level
For additional verses, replace "long legged" with the following:
short legged—hold hands close together
no legged—jump in air

Grade Level: Two

Concept: **Prepare:** A melody may move up, move down, or stay on the same level.

Objectives: Students will

1. sing "Long Legged Sailor" accurately
2. perform a modified clapping pattern with 75 percent accuracy

Materials and Room Preparation:

1. copy of "Long Legged Sailor"
2. large cardboard sailor with adjustable legs
3. pitch pipe

Procedure:

1. Motivation: Present large cardboard sailor. Ask: "What do sailors do?" "What kind of clothes do they wear?" "Who can lengthen the cardboard sailor's legs?" "Who can shorten his legs?"

"I know a song about a sailor. The words will tell you which way to move the sailor's legs."

2. Sequence (whole-song approach)

a. Sing the first verse. Allow the children to respond.

b. Sing the first verse and add the movement indicated by the * in manuscript (spread hands apart). Invite children to imitate your movements.

c. Sing the first verse, adding *, P, and C movements (spread hands apart, pat hands rapidly on thighs, and clap own hands). Discuss these movements with class.

d. Sing the first verse, inviting the children to perform all movements.

e. Sound the starting pitch (F). Invite the children to sing the first verse with movement. Listen and observe. If problems occur, sing the song phrase by phrase and ask the children to echo. Delete the movement if necessary.

Have you ever ever ever in your long legged life,

> (children repeat)

Seen a long legged sailor with his long legged wife?

> (children repeat)

f. When the children can sing the phrases accurately, listen and observe as they sing the song with actions.

Closure: "Tomorrow we'll sing 'Long Legged Sailor' again. We'll learn some more motions and a new verse."

Evaluation Technique: Formative evaluation: Observe the students as they sing and perform motions. Are the students able to sing the song accurately? Can they perform the clapping pattern with 75 percent accuracy?

Preparing a Concept Lesson

Once you feel comfortable with rote song lessons, you are ready to design a lesson that labels or reinforces a concept (see Chapter Ten). If you are like many other beginning teachers, this may seem beyond your ability. Do not despair! Music series books and Chapters Five through Nine of this book offer many excellent suggestions to help you prepare your lessons. The teacher's guides include procedures, charts, pictures, activities, and transparency and ditto masters. Make use of these resources. They are designed for your use.

If for some reason you are unable to use a series book, it will be necessary to design a specific procedure. The following discussion presents ideas to spark your imagination. As you read and reread these ideas, keep your concept and objectives in mind. Remember that at least one phrase of your song should be a *clear* example of the concept that you want to label or reinforce.

One of the best ways to prepare or reinforce a concept is through physical movement. As an example, if your selected concept area is *form*, students can experience and demonstrate the form of a song or composition by imitating your movements or creating appropriate movements of their own. Through key questions such as "Is this phrase or section the *same* or *different?*" and "Should the movement for this phrase or section be the same or different?" you can lead students to discover the form of a song or composition.

If your chosen concept area is *melody*, you can lead students to create a picture of a rising or falling melodic line. Using hands, arms, or bodies, students can depict short melodic phrases. Questions such as "Which way do our hands move when we sing 'Hot Cross Buns'?" will help in the derivation of correct terminology.

Concepts of rhythm can be reinforced by movement or dance steps. One common dance step is a four-beat pattern in which the first three beats are audible steps and the fourth is a silent bend at the knees. The pattern is—step, step, step, bend—step, step, step, bend—and so on. Once the students have enjoyed and danced this step, it is simple to transfer the pattern to hands (clap, clap, clap, rest) and finally to the blackboard as ♩ ♩ ♩ 𝄽.

Instruments provide another useful way to reinforce concepts. Simple rhythmic patterns can be played on rhythm instruments as accompaniment to songs. Young children can begin by playing the beat and later can contrast the beat with the rhythm (the "way the words go") or simple rhythmic ostinati. Step bells or resonator bells are equally useful in melodic learning. Through questions such as "Are these bells different?" and "Will they make a different sound?" students can be led to play familiar phrases and melodies by ear. (Step bells have the additional advantage of functioning as a visual aid in comparing high and low, rising and falling, and steps and leaps.)

Icons are useful in preparing and reinforcing concepts. Pictures representing melodic or rhythmic movement can be placed on blackboard, felt board, or charts. As an example, the teacher or students can arrange pictures of hot cross buns to match the melody of the song.

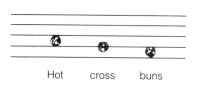

"Maps" can be designed by students to represent concepts from any or all of the concept areas. Rhythm can be notated as dots, dashes, or pictures. The following map represents the melody, rhythm, and form of "Hot Cross Buns."

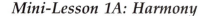

Sample Concept Mini-Lessons

In the following sample lesson plans on labeling or reinforcing a concept, it is assumed that children have, in previous lessons, memorized the songs used in each plan.

In both lessons, an attempt has been made to illustrate varied yet practical approaches to the teaching of musical concepts. Remember, there are an infinite number of right ways to teach a lesson. You are limited only by your imagination.

Mini-Lesson 1A: Harmony

Canoe Song

Grade Level: Five

Concept: Label: Some harmonic textures are homophonic. Some harmonic textures are polyphonic.

Objectives: Students will

1. create a homophonic texture by singing "Canoe Song" with autoharp accompaniment
2. create a polyphonic texture by singing "Canoe Song" as a four-part round
3. identify the textures verbally as homophonic or polyphonic

Materials and Room Preparation:

autoharp

Procedure:

1. Motivation
"Who remembers the words of 'Canoe Song'? (Show of hands.) Raise your hand if you think you can sing the song without a mistake. Let's see if you can sing the song as a group without my help."

2. Sequence
a. Sound starting pitch (A). Strum autoharp and motion group to begin.
b. If students are unable to sing song correctly, review words and melody phrase by phrase.
c. Review: "When we accompany a song with the autoharp, what kind of harmony do we create?" (homophonic)
d. "Today, we'll try another kind of harmony. Sing 'Canoe Song' softly. As you sing, watch what I am doing." (Begin one measure after class starts.) Elicit class response. Allow class to define a round.
e. "Let's try singing 'Canoe Song' as a two-part round." Divide the class into two sections.
f. "That was great! Let's sing the song as a three-part round."
g. "Do you think we could sing a four-part round? Let's try."
h. "We have just created *harmony.* Is it the same as the harmony we created earlier in the lesson?" (no) "How is it different? Harmony that consists of two or more independent melodies sounding together is called *polyphonic.*" Write the word on the board. All pronounce the word together. "The prefix *poly* means *many.* Can you think of other words that begin with *poly?* (polygon, polytechnic, polysyllabic, polyunsaturated)

Closure: "What kind of harmony did we create when we sang 'Canoe Song' with the autoharp?" (homophonic) "What did we create when we sang 'Canoe Song' as a round? (polyphonic) Tomorrow we'll invite our principal in to hear us create homophonic and polyphonic textures."

Evaluation Technique: Formative: Listen and observe. Are students able to sing "Canoe Song" as a round? With autoharp accompaniment? Can they label the textures as homophonic or polyphonic?

Mini-Lesson 2A: Melody

Grade Level: Two

Concept: Transfer: A melody may move up, move down, or stay on the same level.

Objective: Students will demonstrate their understanding of the concept by accurately using hand movements to indicate the melodic shape of "Long Legged Sailor."

Materials and Room Preparation:

step bells and mallet

chart of "Long Legged Sailor"

pitch pipe

tape

Procedure:

1. Motivation
"Let's see who can guess the name of the mystery song for today. Raise your hand if you know the answer." Sing "Long Legged Sailor" on neutral syllable *loo.* Accept response.

2. Sequence
a. Sing song with students. Tape chart of "Long Legged Sailor" on the board.

Long Legged Sailor

b. "Where does the melody move up?" Ask a student to walk up and point. Ask another student to find other examples. Repeat the procedure with "Where does the melody move down?" and "Where does the melody stay on the same level?"

c. "Watch me as I sing the first phrase. What am I doing with my hands?" (using hands to show melodic movement)

d. "Let's all use our hands as we sing 'Long Legged Sailor.' " Sound starting pitch (F) and sing song.

e. "Great! Let's do that again. This time put the melody in your head and let your hands sing the song silently."

f. "Excellent! Let's look at the step bells. The lowest sound in our song is here." Point to F. "To play 'Long Legged Sailor,' which direction will I move first?" (up) "Pretend you have a mallet in your hand. Sing together and pretend to play. When you are finished, I'll choose someone to play the song on the bells." Sound F and begin the song.

g. Observe the students as they play "in the air." Choose several students to play as the class sings.

Closure: "That was fun! Tomorrow I'll bring xylophones and we'll all have a chance to play 'Long Legged Sailor'."

Evaluation Technique: Formative evaluation: Observe as children move their hands and pretend to play step bells. Do all the children move their hands correctly?

The Completed Lesson Plan

When you have written and completed a lesson plan, be sure to check it carefully. Review your lesson objectives and read each step of the procedure. Ask:

Does this step lead my students toward accomplishment of stated objectives?

Does this step lead smoothly into the next?

Did I use the words *explain* or *tell?* Could these words be replaced with questions, visual aids, examples, or activities that would *lead* children to *discover* the answer for themselves?

When you are satisfied with your responses, prepare to teach the lesson.

TEACHING THE LESSON

By now you have completed one or more lesson plans. These plans have been reviewed and are ready for teaching. Are you ready to teach them? Do you know the equipment, materials, and procedures by heart? Will the atmosphere in your classroom be conducive to learning? Are you ready to handle discipline problems? The remainder of this chapter will help you anticipate problems in advance and ultimately acquire the poise and confidence you need to have a positive and rewarding teaching experience.

Classroom Preparation

Before the lesson begins, have the room ready. Allow time during recess or when students are busy with other activities to prepare the equipment and materials for the music lesson. Set up record players, tape recorders, overhead projectors, and screens. Position the piano so that you can see all class members easily. Check that all equipment is operative. Become thoroughly familiar with operating procedures. Have your record in place on the record player, the cassette tape rewound and ready to play, and musical instruments and books sorted and ready for distribution.

Place charts or other visual aids where they can be seen by everyone. Take necessary measures to ensure that charts can be safely and firmly positioned or taped in place for the duration of the lesson.

Enthusiasm and Attitude

Capitalize on the enthusiasm and pleasure that is usually associated with music. Let your facial expressions and movement reflect your own enjoyment, and your students will respond in like manner.

Are you concerned with your voice quality? Don't be! If you are afraid to sing, your fears will transfer to your students, and they will be deprived of the pleasure of music making. Every voice is unique and beautiful. Every voice improves with practice. You and your students can practice together.

Keep class enthusiasm high. Change the room arrangement: Let students gather around the piano, sit together on a rug, or stand in a large circle. As children learn new songs, write key words on brightly colored cards. Staple the cards on a bulletin board or string them around the ceiling. Put on a program for family and friends. Dress up in costumes. Use your imagination and resources.

Presence

Know your music. Practice each song until you can sing it without error. When you can start at the beginning of any phrase with confidence, you are ready to teach your song.

Know your procedure. Review the lesson in your mind until you can go through each step in sequence without looking at your lesson plan. If possible, find a volunteer or group of volunteers who will serve as a practice class.

It is difficult, as an inexperienced teacher, to estimate the time necessary to teach a given lesson. If you must fill a specified period of time, be sure to prepare and include additional activities with your lesson plan.

If you think you will have trouble remembering the sequence or main points of your lesson, construct charts, transparencies, or colorful pictures to use during your lesson. These supports function as visual aids for students and as memory aids for you. Similarly, an autoharp or guitar is an invaluable aid if you feel insecure about your voice quality or ability to stay on pitch. Musical instruments, puppets, charts, and other manipulative aids also give you something to hang on to.

It is normal to feel apprehensive about your first teaching assignment. Even experienced teachers admit that they are frequently nervous before they meet a new class or present a new lesson. If you know your music and procedure well, however, your lesson will go smoothly. Relax! When it is time to teach, step confidently to the front of the room, smile, establish eye contact with the students, wait until you have their attention, and begin. Any initial signs of nervousness will rapidly disappear as you and the students become involved in the lesson.

Discipline

Pause for a few moments now and think about your years in elementary school. Did you participate in music activities, sing in the choir, play in the band? Did you work hard? Have fun? Create disturbances? Did you wish the teacher had been better organized, talked less, accomplished more, handled class disruptions in a consistent manner?

Will your future students wish that you were better prepared or more consistent? Do you know in advance what course of action you will pursue if a problem arises? If a child speaks out-of-turn or bothers another child, what will you do? If a child refuses to participate, what will you do?

Every teacher develops an individual approach to classroom discipline. The following guidelines may prove helpful as you experiment and seek to establish your own management and leadership style.

1. *Be prepared and organized.* Prepare and know the lesson well. Set up and test the equipment in advance. Arrange materials and equipment to avoid unnecessary time loss, movement, and distraction.

2. *Inform students of expected behavior.* Discuss appropriate behavior with the class. Stress that all students have a right to learn and enjoy music without interference from other class members.

3. *Speak clearly and audibly.* Wait until you have the attention of all students before beginning the lesson. Then speak clearly and audibly.

4. *Be consistent.* Before class begins, develop a tentative procedure for handling inappropriate behavior. Discuss the steps with the class. Be consistent and handle each infraction swiftly and immediately. Consider a sequence such as the following:

First infraction:	Child is given verbal warning
Second infraction:	Child assumes different position in the group
Third infraction:	Child is moved to an isolated position
Fourth infraction:	Child is moved out of the room

For most young children, a few moments of isolation from the group is sufficient reminder of the need for self-discipline and control.

5. *Establish eye contact.* Throughout the lesson, focus your eyes and your attention on the class. Avoid staring at ceilings or walls. Avoid turning your back to the class.

6. *Establish routines.* Many discipline problems arise because the teacher has not established efficient routines for distributing materials and moving children in and out of seats. Before class begins, plan consistent ways to pass out and collect materials and move into and out of game and dance formations.

7. *Avoid confrontation.* In initial lessons, avoid confrontation. If a student challenges your authority or refuses to respond, calmly and firmly offer the child a choice. Plan these choices in advance. "Jimmy, turn to page three, or move to the back of the room." *Wait* until the student has made the choice.

8. *Change activities frequently.* Alternate between activities that require concentration and those that are relaxing. Keep the lesson challenging and moving. Provide opportunities for each student to contribute.

9. *Positive approach.* All students need rewards for appropriate behavior and special effort. During the lesson all will manifest some desirable behavior. Reward this behavior generously. Build rewards into the lesson. "If you return to your seats quietly, you can listen to your favorite record." "Let's see who will be a good listener today. Good listeners will be allowed to play a percussion accompaniment with our new song." Be sure that these rewards are, with appropriate effort, attainable by all students.

10. *Listen and observe.* Observe class reaction and response throughout the lesson. Is the class bored? Do the students whisper? Yawn? Are they restless? Perhaps your materials are poorly prepared or inappropriate. Perhaps your lesson is presented in a dull, lifeless, or uninteresting manner. Perhaps you have failed to motivate the students. Make a cassette or videotape of your lesson. Study the tape. Self- and peer-evaluation can help you identify and avoid situations that are potential discipline problems.

EVALUATION

The primary purpose of evaluation is to help you improve yourself or your environment. This section of the chapter will help you improve your teaching performance through development of skills in self- and peer-evaluation.

Self-Evaluation

The first teaching experience is a new, exciting, and sometimes traumatic experience. When you conclude and sit down, you may begin an immediate and critical evaluation of your own performance. You may think you forgot the best parts. Everyone feels the same way! Be kind to yourself. Write down what you did well and what you can improve in your next lesson. Congratulate yourself for preparing and presenting your first lesson and make a mental note to incorporate improvements in the future.

Peer-Evaluation

Peer-evaluation is a valuable source of information, as well as a means of helping you become more aware and better prepared to analyze and evaluate your own lessons. In peer-evaluation, your classmates observe your lesson and, from their own perspectives, offer suggestions for improvement.

Useful and meaningful peer-evaluation requires skill. Your classmates will be acquiring this skill, just as you are, and they will be in different stages of development. It is important, therefore, to study and discuss the following guidelines with your peers *before* evaluation begins.

The Evaluator's Attitude

1. You, as peer-evaluator, are not a judge, nor are you in any way superior. You are an additional source of positive and constructive feedback.

2. You are *learning* a skill. You and the teacher must realize that your evaluation may miss the boat or miss the idea.

3. You are presenting your particular reaction from your particular perspective.

4. Your purpose is not to *change* the teacher. Your purpose is to provide information that can serve as the basis for future change.

The Written or Oral Evaluation

1. Emphasize that your remarks are from your particular perspective. Use statements such as

   It would have helped *me* if . . .

   I believe *I* would have been able to clap the pattern correctly if . . .

   I think I misunderstood your question because . . .

   I felt left out because . . .

   It seemed to me . . .

2. Avoid judgmental statements such as

   You should have . . .

   Don't do this . . .

   You are wrong to . . .

3. When you make suggestions, be constructive and honest. *Always* offer specific suggestions for improvement.

   I was confused when you asked us to play the bells. It would help me if you would begin by demonstrating the proper arm movement.

   I didn't know how to spell the new word. It would have helped me if you had written the word on the board.

4. Organize your comments. Begin with *praise*. Stress the most impressive aspects of the lesson or the teacher's strong points. Next, offer one or two specific suggestions for improvement. Finally, conclude your evaluation with praise. Briefly summarize or restate your opening remarks or describe some part of the presentation in terms of its positive effect on you.

5. Be sensitive to the teacher's needs, personality, and emotional state. Be sure all remarks are relevant to the purpose of the presentation. Avoid comment on situations or conditions over which the teacher has no control.

Lesson Evaluation Form

When you are ready to teach, ask one or more of your classmates to evaluate your lesson. If possible, discuss the lesson with your evaluator. Review the comments as you plan future lessons. A sample evaluation form is provided at the end of this chapter.

SUMMARY

The basic parts of a mini-lesson plan include grade level, concept, lesson objectives, materials, procedures, evaluation technique, and closure. The part of the lesson that provides the initial impulse or incentive to learn is the motivation. The procedure is the series of steps that leads students toward accomplishment of lesson objectives.

Two types of mini-lessons are discussed. In rote song mini-lessons, children learn songs by rote procedures. Concept mini-lessons focus on labeling or reinforcing specific concepts.

Careful preparation precedes the teaching of a mini-lesson. Successful teachers arrange the classroom and test equipment in advance, sort and prepare books and materials, and rehearse and memorize the lesson procedure. They also plan the ways in which they will handle inappropriate student behavior, distribute materials, and move children to and from seated positions.

Peer-evaluation is a valuable source of positive and constructive feedback. Useful and meaningful evaluation, however, requires skill. Evaluators avoid judgmental statements, offer specific suggestions for improvement, begin and end evaluations with praise, and remain sensitive to the needs, personality, and emotional state of each teacher.

SUGGESTED PROJECTS

1. Select a song that is suitable for rote teaching and prepare a rote song mini-lesson. Practice the lesson and teach it to a group of children or peers.

2. Using the same song, prepare a mini-lesson that teaches a concept.

3. Discuss discipline with several experienced teachers. Write a brief essay describing (1) ways you can anticipate and avoid disturbances in the classroom and (2) the steps you will take if discipline problems arise.

4. Group project: Discuss teacher evaluation with a group of your peers. Teach a mini-lesson and ask the group members to make written or oral evaluations.

Lesson Evaluation

Teacher's Name _____   Starting Time _____

Ending Time _____

1. Grade Level

Was this lesson appropriate for the intended grade level? Explain.

2. Procedure

Motivation: Comment on the effectiveness of the motivation. How does it relate to the lesson?

Sequence: Did the lesson flow smoothly from one point to the next? How could the sequence be improved? Explain.

3. Evaluation

What technique was used to evaluate student progress?

4. Closure

How did the ending motivate the class?

5. Preparation

Were materials and necessary equipment prepared in advance? Comment on the efficiency of routines used to distribute materials or move students to and from seated positions.

6. Presence

Did the teacher demonstrate enthusiasm, eye-contact, and discipline? What strong points does this teacher have?

*T*he Music Reading Program

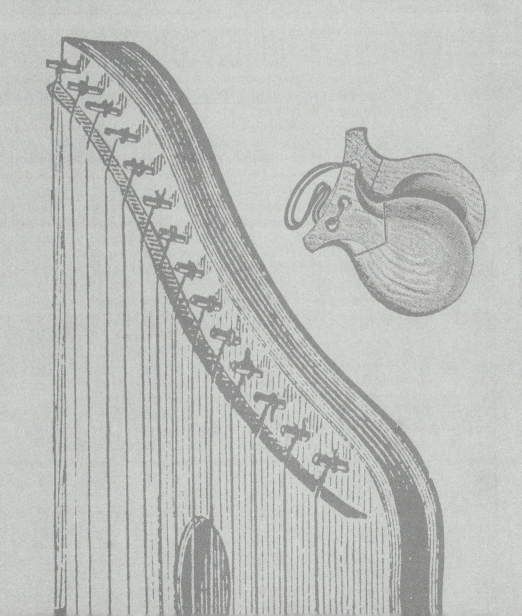

The ability to interpret accurately or understand the meaning of musical notation is a useful and valuable skill. Teachers who are unable to interpret music notation are forever dependent on recordings or friends who are able to sing or play melodies on an instrument. Those who can read music, however, are able to explore easily and independently the many songs and other masterpieces of music available in written notation. For this reason, Part Five introduces two approaches to music education, each of which directly or indirectly leads students toward the development of music reading skills.

Chapter Twelve presents a vocal approach to music literacy, the ability to read, write, and think music. Based on the philosophy of Zoltán Kodály, materials and teaching strategies in this chapter emphasize singing as the primary route to music literacy.

Chapter Thirteen presents an instrumental approach to music literacy. Influenced by the philosophy of Carl Orff, materials and activities in this chapter emphasize speech, movement, and the use of instruments as primary routes toward development of the ability to interpret and understand musical notation.

Chapter Fourteen is a collection of songs to sing, read, or play. These songs, selected from the American heritage, encourage immediate and active participation in music reading.

TWELVE

*M*usic Literacy: A Vocal Approach

"Instruments are available to only a few, but the human voice, the finest of all instruments, free and accessible to everyone, can become the fertile soil for a general musical culture."[1]

As a child you were exposed to music in a variety of ways. Perhaps you listened to music on the radio or had access to records and tapes. Maybe you joined with friends or relatives as they sang at social gatherings or club meetings. As you grew older, you acquired a repertoire of songs that you could sing from memory. Still, you were not musically literate. You could not read or write music.

One of the goals of music education today is music literacy, "the ability to read, write, and think music."[2] When you teach your students a song by rote, you are completing an important first step toward accomplishing this goal. What are the next steps?

This chapter is an overview of a successful vocal approach to music literacy based on the philosophy of Zoltán Kodály (Zōl'-tän Kō'-dī) referred to as the *Kodály method of music education*. The following pages are an introduction to this method and include: (1) the philosophy of Zoltán Kodály, (2) the use of folk songs, (3) tonic sol–fa, (4) rhythm syllables, (5) teaching sequence, and (6) teaching strategy.

THE PHILOSOPHY OF ZOLTÁN KODÁLY

Zoltán Kodály was born in Kecskemet, Hungary, on December 16, 1882. His father, an employee of the railroads, was a violinist, and his mother was a pianist and singer. As a child, he took piano and violin lessons and spent many evenings playing chamber music with his family.

With the help of his parents, Kodály developed a high degree of music literacy. He joined the school orchestra and, while still in school, wrote his first orchestral composition. The work received a successful performance in 1898, and Kodály continued to compose vocal and orchestral music throughout his life.

As a young man, Kodály became interested in the music of the Hungarian peasants. In 1905, he personally collected over 150 folk melodies. These songs, which he later described as "small masterpieces" of music, would eventually serve as the basis for intensive study and a doctoral dissertation on the structure of Hungarian folk song.

Kodály received his teaching diploma in 1905 and began lecturing at the Academy of Music in Budapest in 1907. As the years passed, he became increasingly aware of the poor condition of public music education in Hungary. Though many of the rural peasants could sing Hungarian folk songs, very few could read or write music. Kodály observed and was saddened by this lack of music literacy. He wrote:

> Hungarian society, which can very well distinguish between inferior and vintage wines, drinks inferior wine in music. No wonder that at most five thousand people go to the Opera House and a thousand or two to concerts. Or that the more valuable the programme the emptier the concert hall.[3]

As a result of his observations, Kodály began a campaign aimed at the creation of a musically literate Hungarian society. He worked vigorously to improve the music education of future teachers. He pressed for the introduction of tonic sol–fa (a method of reading music by using syllables), prepared public addresses, wrote numerous essays, and actively advocated the establishment of Hungarian folk music as the foundation of Hungarian music education. Furthermore, he urged government authorities to introduce music education in early childhood. He advocated that this education be approached through the instrument most accessible to everyone, the human voice.

Kodály lived to see many of his ideals and beliefs put into practice. In the years between 1950 and 1960, more than 100 musical primary schools, where music is taught on a daily basis, opened in Hungary. As these children learned how to think, read, and write music, the Hungarian population began to develop the music literacy that Kodály had envisioned so many years before.

THE KODÁLY METHOD

Today Kodály's tenets have spread far beyond the Hungarian borders. His pupils and followers have created a method that is used in many parts of the world. The following pages explore this method as it has been adapted for use in American schools.

Use of Folk Songs

You may recall singing "Yankee Doodle," "Skip to My Lou," "Clementine," "Ezekiel Saw the Wheel," and "On Top of Old Smoky." These songs are part of the American folk song heritage. **Folk songs** are often casually defined as music "of the people, by the people, and for the people." Actually, this definition is reasonably accurate. Passed from generation to generation, folk songs are the musical tradition and heritage of regions or communities. Unlike music that has been composed by an individual, folk music is a product of the many people who have sung, varied, edited, and passed it to succeeding generations.

Folk songs from the student's musical heritage form the basic repertoire of the Kodály method of music education. Short and often repetitive, these songs are an excellent resource for classroom use. As music literacy develops, the musical repertoire expands to include composed music and folk songs of other cultures and nations.

Tonic Sol–Fa

When children can perform a basic repertoire of folk songs from their own cultural heritage, they are introduced to tonic sol–fa. Tonic sol–fa, a system adapted from earlier methods by John Curwen in nineteenth-century England, functions as a tool in the development of music literacy. With practice, use of tonic sol–fa enables students to perceive, identify, and label sound relationships. Thus it is an invaluable aid in the development of the ability to think, read, and write music.

In the tonic sol–fa system, each step or note of a scale (see p. 110) is associated with a syllable. The syllables associated with the major scale are *dō, rĕ, mĭ, fă, sōl, lă,* and *tĭ.* The G major scale is sung in tonic sol–fa as follows:

do   re   mi   fa   sol   la   ti   do

Normally only the initial consonants of each syllable are used in notation. The eighth step of the scale is sung *do* but is referred to as *high do* and is written *d'*.

The home tone, or *tone center*, of major scales (see p. 117) is always *do*. Thus the tonic sol–fa system is sometimes referred to as *movable do*. Compare the following examples:

G major scale

F major scale

Minor scales have *la* as the tone center. Compare the following:

E natural minor scale

D natural minor scale

In notation, a subscript is added to syllables below *do*. The first step of the minor scale is sung as *la* but is referred to as *low la* and is written *l*.

In the system of John Curwen, each syllable is associated with a hand sign. Hand signs are performed in front of the body. As a melody rises, the hand rises accordingly. As a melody falls, the hand is lowered.

Curwen-Kodály
hand signs

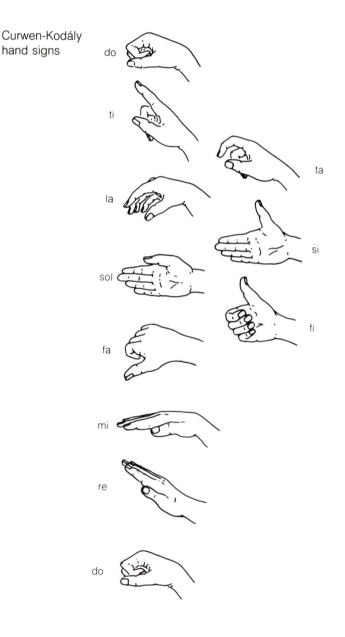

do

ti

ta

la

si

sol

fi

fa

mi

re

do

Hand signs function as a visual and physical link between sounds and symbols. The visualization of sound relationships in space serves as an important aid in the development of aural perception and in-tune singing. The use of hand signs provides an opportunity for active physical participation in sound production.

Rhythm Syllables

Syllables are also used in the development of the ability to read and interpret rhythm patterns. These syllables, referred to as *rhythm syllables,* enable students to verbalize the duration of sounds. The following list includes several of the rhythm syllables in common use:[4]

Rhythm syllables

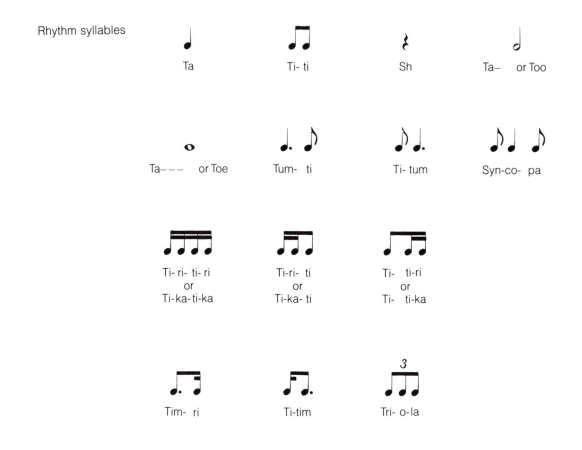

Initially, rhythm syllables are presented apart from the music staff. For ease in writing, note heads are often eliminated. This type of notation is called stick notation and is illustrated below. You will encounter other examples of stick notation in Chapter Thirteen.

Stick notation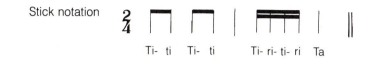

Ti- ti   Ti- ti   Ti- ri- ti- ri   Ta

Teaching Sequence

Tonic sol–fa and rhythm syllables are introduced to children in a carefully planned sequence. Based on the age and general developmental level of children, this teaching order begins with the syllables that are associated with the tone-calls of early childhood (see p. 21). Recall for a moment the tone-calls you heard and sang as a child (see also p. 22). The short calls were probably similar to the following:

We know some-thing you don't know!

John-ny has a girl friend!

In syllables, these calls are

s s m m s s m

s s m l s m

The sol–fa syllables *so, mi,* and *la* and the rhythm syllables *ta* and *ti-ti* are among the first syllables introduced to children.

The following chart, though not all-inclusive, illustrates a suggested order for the introduction of sol–fa and rhythm syllables. It is assumed that this sequence will be introduced gradually over a period of years, the length of time depending on the frequency of music instruction.

Sol–fa Syllables	Rhythm Syllables
s and m	ta
l	ti-ti
d	sh
r	too
l,	toe
s,	tum-ti, ti-tum
d'	syn-co-pa
f	ti-ri-ti-ri
	ti-ti-ri, ti-ri-ti
t	tim-ri
	tri-o-la

Teaching Strategy

Sol–fa and rhythm syllables in this teaching order are presented through teaching strategies (see p. 154). As you will recall from Chapter Ten, a teaching strategy is a long-range plan designed to enable students to master a concept. In the Kodály approach, a teaching strategy is used to introduce each syllable or pattern of syllables in the teaching order. Thus, over a period of years, children are led gradually toward the attainment of music literacy.[5]

To help you understand the nature of teaching strategies as they are used in the Kodály approach, let us assume that you are planning to introduce *s,* (*low sol*) to your class. Because you are following the teaching order, your class is already proficient with *s, m, l, d, r,* and *l,.* Let us further assume that you have selected the syllable pattern d–l,–s,. This pattern occurs frequently in American folk songs.

Your objectives are to design a strategy that will enable students to (1) recognize the patterns d–l,–s, aurally and visually and (2) perform and notate this pattern correctly.

Your first task will be to select songs and activities for the preparation stage of the strategy (see p. 154). Depending on the age and developmental level of your class, you may select songs such as "Turn Your Glasses Over," "Mama Don't 'Low," "Bought Me a Dog," "Chicken Ma Craney Crow," "This Train," and "Sourwood Mountain." The following examples are excerpts from these songs:

Turn Your Glasses Over (excerpt)

Mama Don't 'Low (excerpt)

Ma - ma don't 'low no mu - sic play - in' round here, _____

Bought Me a Dog (excerpt)

Bought me a dog, bought me a cat, They both fight but I don't mind that,

Chicken Ma Craney Crow (excerpt)

Chick - en ma chick - en my cra - ney crow,

This Train (excerpt)

This train is bound for glo - ry, This train,_____

Sourwood Mountain (excerpt)

Chick - en crow - in' on Sour - wood Moun - tain,

In the preparation stage, students will be given many experiences with songs containing the pattern d–l,–s,. They will learn these songs by rote (see p. 38). As yet, they will not see or discuss the symbols. They may, however, create pictorial representations (icons) of a melodic phrase or use hands to shape the rise and fall of a melody (see p. 155).

When children can perform the activities and sing the preparation songs accurately, the teacher introduces the symbols. This is the labeling stage. You may want to write "Turn Your Glasses Over" on the board in music notation and lead children to discover the new note (s,).

d   d   d   l,   ?

The new note is labeled as *s*, and the correct placement of the hand sign (below *l*,) is demonstrated.

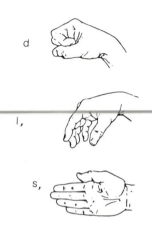

In the transfer stage, the preparation songs are reviewed. Children locate the phrases with *s*, and sing these phrases with hand signs in sol–fa, and write the phrases in music notation. In addition, they identify and perform the d–l,–s, pattern in new and unfamiliar songs and create their own melodies using d–l,–s,.

In the evaluation stage, the teacher checks to see that objectives have been met (see p. 156). This can be accomplished in many different ways. You may choose to test aural recognition of d–l,–s, by singing a phrase on a neutral syllable (*loo*) and asking the class to sing the phrase in sol–fa. You can further test students' ability to notate by asking them to write this same phrase in music notation. Visual recognition of d–l,–s, and the students' ability to perform this pattern can be measured by asking the class to sing a new song from notation, without help from the teacher. If the students can perform accurately, they are ready to begin a new strategy.

The Kodály Method in Your Classroom

The Kodály approach is comprehensive and based on a carefully sequenced collection of songs and materials. Current music series books contain sol–fa and rhythm syllable guides, songs and activities, and suggestions for incorporating the Kodály method into the elementary classroom. Many fine workshops and summer courses are available throughout the United States and Canada. The reading list at the end of this chapter will provide you with additional information and lead you to appropriate materials. Make use of these fine resources and guide your students toward Kodály's dream of universal music literacy.

It is not worth much if we sing for ourselves; it is finer if two sing together, then more and more people—hundreds, thousands, until the great Harmony rings forth in which all of us can be united.[6]

SUMMARY

The Kodály method, based on the philosophy of Zoltán Kodály (1882–1967), is a successful approach to music literacy, the ability to read, write, and think music. Kodály believed that education was a means for all people to develop an appreciation and enjoyment of music. He insisted that music education be introduced in early childhood and approached through the instrument most accessible to everyone, the human voice.

Folk songs from the students' musical heritage form the basic repertoire of the Kodály method. As music literacy develops, repertoire expands to include composed music and folk songs of other cultures and nations.

Tonic sol–fa and rhythm syllables function as tools in the development of music literacy. Each step or note of a scale is associated with a syllable and a corresponding hand sign. Rhythm syllables enable students to verbalize durations of sounds.

Learning in the Kodály approach is carefully planned and sequenced through use of teaching order and teaching strategies, which are used to introduce each syllable or pattern of syllables. Most current music series books contain sol–fa and rhythm syllable guides, songs and activities, and teaching suggestions for use in teaching via the Kodály approach.

NOTES

1. Ferenc Bonis, ed., *Visszatekintes* (Budapest: Zenemukiado, 1964), p. 4.

2. Lois Choksy, *The Kodály Context* (Englewood Cliffs, N.J.: Prentice–Hall, 1981), p. 6.

3. Zoltán Kodály, *The Selected Writings of Zoltán Kodály* (New York: Boosey and Hawkes, 1974), p. 119.

4. Lois Choksy, op. cit., p. 191.

5. Lois Choksy, authority on the Kodály approach, uses the terms *prepare, make conscious, reinforce,* and *assess* to describe the four stages of a teaching strategy.

6. Ferenc Bonis, op. cit., p. 200.

SUGGESTED READING

Choksy, Lois. *The Kodály Context: Creating an Environment for Musical Learning*. Englewood Cliffs, N.J.: Prentice–Hall, 1981.

Choksy, Lois. *The Kodály Method: Comprehensive Music Education from Infant to Adult*. Englewood Cliffs, N.J.: Prentice–Hall, 1974.

Daniel, Katinka. *Kodály Approach, Method Book One*. Champaign, Ill.: Mark Foster Music Company, 1979.

Szonyi, Erzsebet. *Kodály's Principles in Practice*. New York: Boosey and Hawkes, 1973.

Young, Percy. *Zoltán Kodály*. London: Ernest Benn Limited, 1964.

THIRTEEN

*M*usic Literacy:
An Instrumental Approach

This chapter is a guide to the use of instruments as a springboard for the development of music literacy—the ability to read, write, and think music. The sequential program presented in the following pages begins with simple accompaniments suitable for reading and playing on nonpitched percussion instruments. It progresses to ostinati and short melodies to be played on pitched instruments such as bells, xylophones, metallophones, and recorders.

Playing musical instruments often motivates students to master note reading. Therefore, the program outlined in this chapter capitalizes on this motivational factor through the integration of music reading with instrumental activities. The approach reflects the influence of the German composer and pedagogue Carl Orff. It relies heavily on a background of rhythmic chanting and body movement along with the playing of instruments as a necessary foundation for the development of music literacy.

CARL ORFF

Carl Orff (1895–1982) pursued two careers during most of his adult life, developing an international reputation as both a composer and an educator. Compositions such as *Carmina Burana* are performed in concert halls around the world. The educational philosophy and materials expressed in Orff's

Musik für Kinder (Music for Children) have greatly influenced the methods and materials used in children's music education throughout Western Europe and North America.

In the years after World War II, Carl Orff, working with another music educator, Gunild Keetman, began to develop ideas and techniques for use with young children. Taking words, movements, chants, and songs that were a natural part of children's own experience, Orff suggested ways to use these as building blocks for musical development. Collaborating with a German manufacturer, he supervised the making of pitched percussion instruments of high quality that could be used by children to improvise accompaniments for chanting, singing, and movement. Between 1950 and 1954, *Musik für Kinder*, a five-volume collection of instrumental, chanting, and singing activities, was developed by Orff and Keetman and published in Germany by Schott.

The first chants suggested by Orff and Keetman are based on the vocabulary of young children: their own names and the names of friends, pets, streets, and places, or any other words children know and like. From this rhythmic chanting, children progress to chanting groups of related words or phrases and finally to rhymes. As soon as a chant is developed, it is accompanied by appropriate rhythm patterns that are performed with body sounds or on percussion instruments.

After children are able to use body sounds such as clapping, snapping, patsching, and stamping as accompaniments for chanting and singing, they play simple two-tone rhythm patterns on mallet instruments with removable bars. These specially designed instruments allow beginning students to play simple accompaniments quickly and easily. Initially, bordurs or two-note ostinati are played with two mallets. Eventually, three-pitch ostinati are played. Accompaniments gradually become more and more complex.

Improvisation lessons, in which children make up their own accompaniments, melodies, and patterns, are begun after a repertoire of spoken chants, rhythm patterns, simple songs, and ostinati has been learned. Some of the early improvisations are based on patterns practiced first in *echo clapping* and then used by children as their "answers" to rhythmic questions. Here are two examples of these activities:

Little by little, children are encouraged to improvise their own (1) chants, (2) rhythmic accompaniments for chants, rhymes, or songs, and (3) ostinati based on a given set of pitches. To ensure a successful musical experience, teachers usually define the parameters for each of these activities.

A careful look at the materials and activities contained in modern series textbooks, as well as a perusal of brochures that advertise classroom instruments sold in the United States and Canada, will reveal the remarkable influence of Carl Orff. Elementary music textbooks acknowledge his contributions and include chanting, improvisation, and music for mallet instruments based on the Orff approach. Every large classroom instrument manufacturer has a line of percussion instruments modeled on those Orff developed in Germany. These techniques and materials offer children opportunities to develop their understanding of music as they create and perform. This chapter uses Orff's method as a foundation for musical literacy.

READING ACTIVITIES WITH NONPITCHED INSTRUMENTS

In preparation for their first reading lessons, children should participate in much chanting, clapping, tapping, moving, and rote playing to develop a repertoire of rhythm patterns that they can recognize aurally. They must be able to perceive aurally the various aspects of rhythm: beat, meter, and rhythm patterns.

The first step in the reading program involves the rote learning of rhythm patterns, followed by presentation of these patterns in notation. This introduction of the notation corresponds with the labeling stage in concept development (see p. 78). Next, children are asked to recognize and perform rhythm patterns as they occur in accompaniments and compositions previously learned by rote. Eventually, they are able to play these patterns in new and unfamiliar music and use them in improvisation and composition. These activities correspond with the transfer stage in concept development.

Stick Notation

Most recent elementary music textbook series begin rhythmic reading with simple rhythm patterns represented by stick notation. In this system, sounds lasting for one beat are notated with the symbol

| | | |

tah tah tah tah

Sounds occurring two to a beat are represented by the symbol

⊓ ⊓ ⊓ ⊓

ti ti ti ti ti ti ti ti

Silences lasting for a whole beat are notated in this manner:

𝄾   𝄾   𝄾   𝄾

Initial encounters with these rhythmic symbols can grow out of spoken chant. After children have developed a rhythmic approach to speaking a chant, they can both clap and speak the chant. Next, they can play the rhythm of the chant on nonpitched percussion instruments. The third step is to share the symbols for the rhythm of the chant with the children and ask them to play as they follow the symbols with their eyes.

Here is a chant based on names of trees.

Pine tree, ash tree,
    Fir tree, beech,
Maple tree, walnut tree,
    Willow tree, peach.

These are the rhythmic symbols for this chant:

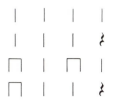

Using the four groups of symbols representing the chant, do the following. Write each of the four groups of stick notation on a separate large card; place the cards in the order in which their notation occurs in the chant, and ask the children to play them. Next, change the order of the cards and ask the children to play the resulting rhythms. These and similar exercises can be practiced with many simple chants, including some presented earlier in this text.

Accompaniments for Chants and Songs

On the coming pages you will find a series of accompaniments arranged in order from simple to more complex. They are notated with stick notation.

A rhythmic accompaniment for the following chant can be created by playing on a drum* this pattern:

and by playing on sticks this pattern:

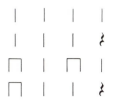

---

*Any accompaniment for nonpitched percussion instruments can be performed with body sounds if instruments are not available.

The Woodchuck

How much wood could a woodchuck chuck
    If a woodchuck could chuck wood?
Lots of wood could a woodchuck chuck
    If the woodchuck could chuck wood.

Here is a percussion accompaniment for the "Old King Cole" chant:

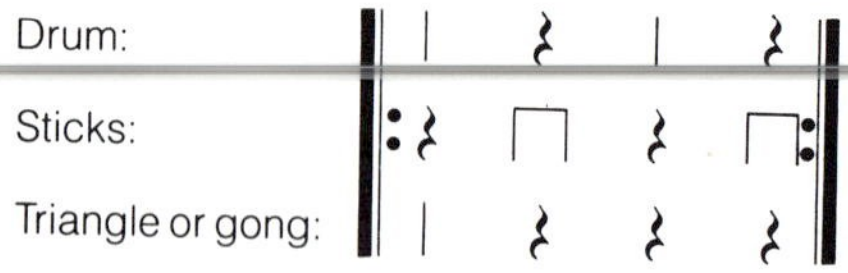

Old King Cole

Old King Cole was a merry old soul,
    And a merry old soul was he.
He called for his pipe and he called for his bowl
    And he called for his fiddlers three.

These accompaniments can be used for other chants in duple meter. (In duple meter, beats move in twos or fours.)

Here is an accompaniment for chants in triple meter. (In triple meter, beats move in threes.)

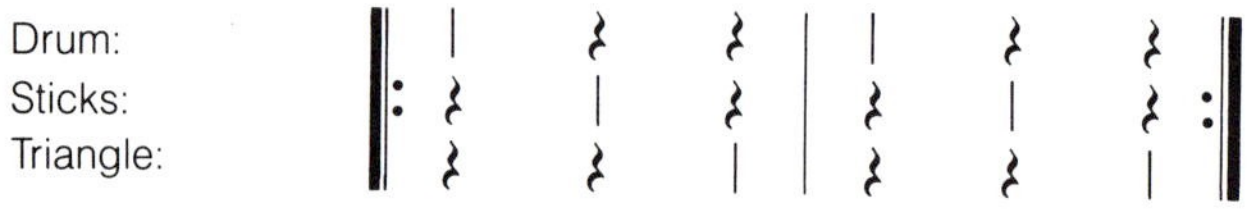

Strawberries, blackberries,
    Raspberries, grapes.
Dewberries, blueberries,
    Gooseberries, dates.

Find other chants in triple meter and accompany them with the above rhythm patterns.

The traditional Hawaiian chant "Aia o Pele i Hawaii" can be accompanied with the following patterns.

Aia o Pele i Hawaii

Traditional

1. A-i -a-la'o Pe - le ı Ha-wai-i, e - a! Ke ha-a ma-i la-i Ma-u-ke-le, e - a!
2. U -hi-u ha-ma-i a - na, e - a! Ke no-me a-e i-a na_ Pu-na, e - a!

1. Pe-le is here in Ha-wai-i, e-a!
   And she is danc-ing in Ma-u-ke-le, e-a!

2. There is grumb-ling la-va that bel-ches, e-a!
   It comes down swal-low-ing the land of Pu-na, e-a!

A colorful accompaniment for the following sea chantey is made up of these patterns:

Turn Your Glasses Over

England

I've been to Har - lem, I've been to Do - ver. I've tra - veled this wide world all o - ver,

O - ver, o - ver, three times o - ver. Drink what you have to drink and

turn your glas - ses o - ver. Sail - ing east, sail - ing west, sail - ing o - ver the o - cean.

Bet - ter look out when the boat be - gins to rock, or you'll lose your girl in the o - cean.

The previous accompaniments require each player to read only one or two rhythm symbols. The patterns of the next accompaniments involve the players in reading combinations of all three of the rhythm symbols presented thus far. Experiment with different ways to recite the following chant expressively as you accompany it with the percussion patterns presented here.

Pease Porridge

Pease porridge hot!

Pease porridge cold!

Pease porridge in the pot,

Nine days old!

Percussion instruments are often used to accompany African songs. Here are some patterns that will add to the enjoyment of singing "Ev'rybody Loves Saturday Night."

Ev'rybody Loves Saturday Night

Standard Notation

It will not take long to transfer from stick notation to standard notation if you and your children have been playing rhythmic patterns successfully. In newer textbook series, children are asked to read simple patterns from traditional notation as early as second grade. The music reading sequence begins with the presentation of quarter notes as symbols that can represent sounds lasting for one beat. Eighth notes, symbols representing two equal sounds per beat, are introduced next. In both of these instances, the traditional notes can be related to their equivalents in stick notation. The rest symbol that is used in the stick notation becomes a slightly more ornate symbol in standard notation.

Here is a percussion accompaniment for a jump-rope chant, presented in standard notation. Notice that the time signature is simplified somewhat. This is a practice followed in most of the newer textbooks.

Down in the valley where the green grass grows,
There sat Cindy* as sweet as a rose.
Along came Johnny* to kiss her on the cheek.
How many kisses do you think he could sneak?
One, two, three, four, five, six, seven, ...

If the transition to standard notation poses difficulties for your class, you might try writing a few patterns on the board in standard notation and placing stick notation underneath. Let the children practice from the stick notation a few times; then erase the stick notation and ask them to read the standard notation.

Here are a few simple patterns in both stick and standard notation. They can be used to accompany most songs in duple meter.

---

*Any names can be used in this chant.

The following patterns can be used to accompany a folk song from Louisiana, "Sweet Potato."

Older children might enjoy adding this third percussion part based on the syncopated pattern at the end of the song.

Sweet Potato

U.S.

Come and get your sweet po-ta-to, sweet po-ta-to, sweet po-ta-to

Come and get your sweet po-ta-to. Watch out! It's ver-y hot.

Children also need to practice reading rhythm patterns in triple meter. Here is an accompaniment for "The Cuckoo" (p. 28).

READING ACTIVITIES WITH PITCHED INSTRUMENTS

Children can begin note-reading activities involving both pitch and rhythm after they understand melodic concepts (see Chapter Seven) and have acquired a repertoire of rhythm patterns that they can play from notation. Newer series textbooks approach the teaching of melodic notation in slightly different ways, but whatever the exact procedures are, they are predicated on the ability to perceive melodic direction. At first, children may be asked to associate spatial relationships with higher and lower pitches on a staff. Next, they may be invited to determine the direction of a short melodic idea notated on a staff. At the same time, children may be asked to accompany familiar songs with one- or two-note instrumental ostinati (for which the letter names of the pitches are given). Often pictures of specific resonator or melody bells to be used in performing the patterns are included above or beside the melodic notation. Arrows may indicate the sequence in which they are to be played.

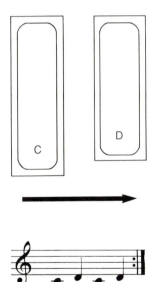

If recorders are used, pictures of the fingerings of the proper pitches are usually given to assist the children as they master both playing and note reading.

Beginning in the fourth grade, children can be expected to read short melodies from standard notation and perform them on recorders or pitched percussion instruments. With a background of rhythmic patterns and an understanding of melodic movement, children have only one new element to deal with: learning the pitch names assigned to lines and spaces on the staff. These letter names are then presented as children are asked to use them, beginning with two or three pitches and progressing until all the lines and spaces of the treble staff are covered.

In the rest of this chapter you will find materials and activities presented in a sequence that will help elementary school students improve their note reading and instrument playing. The playing and improvising of ostinati can be introduced as early as first grade. Some primary grade children are able to play entire melodies from notation on simple pitched instruments. The emphasis on instrumental reading, however, usually begins in the fourth grade.

Ostinati for Pitched Instruments

As you read this section, you will find ostinati that are typically used as accompaniments to folk songs. They are similar to the ostinati and other simple accompaniments in the newer textbook series. When you practice them or try them in your classroom, remember the hints given in Chapter Four regarding two-mallet technique (see p. 53). Body movements should precede the actual playing of ostinati on pitched-bar instruments or improvised instruments such as tuned water glasses.

Either one or both of the ostinati presented here can be used to accompany "Mama Don't 'Low."

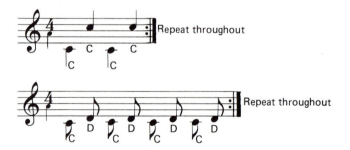

Mama Don't 'Low

U.S.

Ma-ma don't 'low no mu-sic play-in' round here,_____ Ma-ma don't 'low no
mu-sic play-in' round here._____ I don't care what Ma-ma don't 'low, gon-na
play my mu-sic an-y-how, Ma-ma don't 'low no mu-sic play-in' round here._____

"Sourwood Mountain" (p. 31) can be accompanied by this ostinato:

F C D C

Here is an ostinato to be played with "Pretty Saro" (p. 244)

B C D D

Improvisation and Notation

Many children are more interested in learning to use and interpret notation if that task is related to music they have created. One way to capitalize on this interest is to encourage students to improvise short ostinati for chants, rhymes, or songs that are based on pentatonic scales. Improvisation can be done by small groups, by an individual at a music center, or by all students in a larger group. A characteristic of pentatonic ostinati and melodies is that they usually sound well together. (Songs based on pentatonic scales are identified for you in teacher's editions of series texts.) After children have practiced their melodies several times, they should be invited to notate them. This notation can be simplified, based on stick symbols at first, then transformed into regular notation on a staff at a later time.

Toraji

Korea

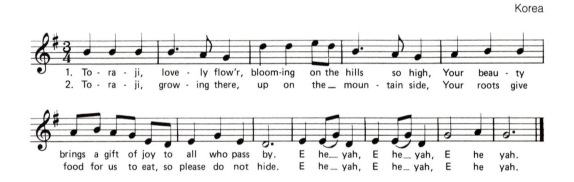

1. To - ra - ji,　love - ly flow'r, bloom-ing　on the hills　so high,　Your　beau - ty
2. To - ra - ji,　grow - ing there,　up　on　the — moun - tain side,　Your　roots give

brings a gift of joy to　all　who pass　by.　E　he — yah,　E　he — yah,　E　he　yah.
food for us　to eat, so please do not hide.　E　he — yah,　E　he — yah,　E　he　yah.

When children can sing "Toraji" successfully, invite them to improvise ostinati using the pitches G–A–B or D–E. You might suggest that they select rhythm patterns from the song for their improvised melodies and notate the patterns with this stick notation:

| | | | | | |　　or　　| ⊓ | | | ⊓ |

Students can indicate pitches later by writing the appropriate letter names (taken from those marked on the bars or bells*) at the bottom of each stick symbol, as in the following example.

The chants and rhymes presented on pages 208–210 can also be accompanied by ostinati improvised and then notated by children. You can help define parameters for rhythm patterns by having your class clap patterns from the board or from large flash cards in the meter appropriate for each chant or rhyme. After this experience, children can base their ostinati on similar patterns.

Independent Melodies for Pitched Instruments

Here are some simple folk melodies that can be played as part of an instrumental music reading program. For use in the classroom, the melodies can be notated on a large chart, projected on a screen by an opaque projector, or transferred to transparencies for use with an overhead projector. The melodies can also be used as part of individual or small group projects prepared in a music center and later shared with the rest of the class.

Notation of these short compositions has been limited to three symbols: quarter notes, eighth notes, and quarter rests. Thus the rhythmic performance can be related directly to earlier activities in which children have used these same symbols. Each melody is notated in two keys, one suitable for reading on pitched bar instruments and the other for soprano recorders.

---

*If children are using tuned water glasses, cards with the letter names of the pitches should be placed in front of the glasses to serve as visual guides.

Hot Cross Buns

Traditional

Hot Cross Buns

Traditional

Whistle, Daughter, Whistle

U.S.

Whistle, Daughter, Whistle

U.S.

The Bee

Germany

The Bee

Germany

Winter, Goodby

Germany

Winter, Goodby

Germany

A Final Word

It is possible for children to gain a basic understanding of musical elements and to develop some performance and creative skills without learning to read music. However, the ability to interpret and perform simple melodies and rhythm patterns from notation facilitates a deeper understanding and enjoyment of music. In addition, the ability to read music gives students an independent means of learning new music throughout their lives. Therefore, the inclusion of a music reading component in the music education program is highly desirable.

The authors believe that the help provided by this book, plus the excellent materials and teaching suggestions found in the series texts, will enable you to plan and direct music reading activities. If you feel that your own ability to interpret notation is not developed, you can practice and improve along with your students.

SUMMARY

One approach to the development of an ability to understand and interpret musical notation is to make that learning process an extension of activities involving the use of instruments. However, children should not be expected to begin to read music and play instruments simultaneously without having had many chanting, singing, music listening, moving, and rote playing experiences. The approach suggested in this chapter reflects the influence of the German composer and educator Carl Orff. Orff believed that words, movements, chants, and songs are the building blocks for musical development.

Initial encounters with a simplified form of rhythmic notation, stick notation, can grow out of spoken chants and songs. The rhythm patterns of the syllables can be notated and clapped and then performed on percussion instruments. Patterns formed with a few words or syllables can be isolated, notated, and performed as accompaniments for chants. Simple accompaniments for songs can also be notated with stick notation and performed on percussion instruments.

Children can be expected to read notation involving both pitch and rhythm after they have developed a repertoire of rhythm patterns they can read and play. Melodic reading should be preceded by the kinds of listening, singing, moving, creating, and playing experiences suggested in Chapter Seven.

Initial melodic notation lessons should include the playing of simple ostinati that are found in series textbooks or presented by the teacher, as well as those created by the students themselves. As children gain confidence in their ability to read and interpret notation, they can begin to play entire melodies on pitched-bar instruments or soprano recorders.

SUGGESTED PROJECTS

1. Create and notate percussion accompaniments for three poems or nursery rhymes appropriate for a grade of your choice.

2. Compare the approaches to rhythmic reading presented in two of the newer second-grade series texts. Is there a special section devoted to instrumental reading? Are the rhythm patterns related to songs or rhymes that would be enjoyed by children?

3. Prepare a collection of pentatonic songs for use with ostinati improvised on Orff-type mallet instruments.

4. Prepare a collection of melodies for children to read on melody instruments. Be sure that every note is within the range of available melody instruments.

FOURTEEN

Songs to Sing, Read, and Play

Is your singing voice out of practice? The following song collection has been chosen for you. You will find traditional songs from the American heritage, singing games, part songs, partner songs, rounds, and more. These songs are fun to sing and popular with teachers and children, and the texts and games encourage immediate and active participation.

This collection can be explored in a number of ways. You may (1) learn the songs by rote, (2) play the songs on a recorder, (3) create appropriate accompaniments, (4) play the games or add action, (5) follow the teaching suggestions, and (6) read the songs in sol–fa and rhythm syllables (see p. 197). Chord symbols, where appropriate, are written above the music manuscript of each song, and a summary of the sol–fa syllables, with the tone centers circled, is included for practicing reading music.

As an aid for the beginning teacher, selections are arranged in order by grade level. Songs suitable for kindergarten and grade one begin on page 224, grade two on page 231, grades three and four on page 235, and grades five and six on page 241. This arrangement is a general guide. Most of the songs can be used with equal success in various grades. Enjoy!

Lemonade

When the class is familiar with this song, select a child to sing the parts marked *1*. The group responds by singing the parts marked *2*.

Rain, Rain Go Away

Rain, rain go a-way, Come a-gain some o-ther day.

Hot Cross Buns

Hot cross buns, Hot cross buns, One a-pen-ny two a-pen-ny, Hot cross buns.

John Kanaka

I heard, I heard the old man say, John Ka-na-ka na-ka Too-la-ay, Today, to-day is a hol-i-day, John Ka-na-ka na-ka Too-la-ay.
Too-la-ay, Too-la-ay, John Ka-na-ka na-ka Too-la-ay.

From *The Kodály Context: Creating an Environment for Musical Learning* by Lois Choksy. Copyright 1981 by Prentice-Hall, Inc. Reprinted by permission.

1. Children form double circle with boys on outside and girls on inside.
2. Girls face the boys and establish partners.
3. On phrase one ("I heard, I heard, ..."), boys do-si-do around their female partners.
4. On "John," children stamp foot.
   On "Kanaka naka," tap knees in rhythm.
   On "Toola," clap own hands twice.
   On "ay," clap partner's hands once.
5. On "Today, today . . . ," repeat do-si-do with partner.
6. Repeat step 4.
7. On "Too-la-ay, too-la-ay," boys step to the left to establish a new partner (children may also do "Too-la-ay" clap pattern as they walk).
8. Children repeat step 4, and game begins again with the new partners.

Old MacDonald

s, l, d r m

Traditional

Chicken Ma Craney Crow

s, l, (d) r m

Mississippi

Chick-en ma chick-en my cra-ney crow, I went to the well to wash my toe,

When I got back my black eyed chick-en was gone. What time old witch? 1! (spoken)

Transcribed from Archive of Folk Song Recording AFS 6657, Library of Congress, Washington, D.C.

Formation   Line of "Chickens" with "Hen" as last person in line.

□□□□□□□□□□□□□□○

Hawk

Action   Each child, in turn, sings the song, increasing the spoken number by a predetermined amount (five minutes, ten minutes, an hour, etc.).

Hawk watches as each child sings. When the last child has sung, Hen asks Hawk, "What are you looking for?"

Hawk replies, "I'm looking for a needle."

Hen holds up parts of the body (arm, leg, elbow, etc.) and asks, "Is this it?" Hawk replies "no" each time.

When Hen points to the head, Hawk replies "yes," Hen cries "squat," Chickens squat or scatter, and Hawk attempts to catch or tag a standing player to be the next Hawk.

Jolly Old Saint Nicholas

s, l, (d) r m

Traditional

Jol - ly old Saint Nich - o - las, Lean your ear this way; Don't you tell a sin - gle soul What I'm going to say; Christ-mas Eve is com - ing soon, Now, you dear old man, Whis - per what you'll bring to me, Tell me, if you can.

2. When the clock is striking twelve,
   When I'm fast asleep,
   Down the chimney broad and black
   With your pack you'll creep;
   All the stockings you will find
   Hanging in a row,
   Mine will be the shortest one,
   You'll be sure to know.

Hey Betty Martin

s, l, t, (d) r m

Hey, Bet - ty Mar - tin, tip-py toe, tip-py toe, Hey, Bet - ty Mar - tin, tip - toe fine.

Hey, Bet - ty Mar - tin, tip-py toe, tip-py toe, Hey, Bet - ty Mar - tin, Please be mine.

1. Ask children to step the beat, changing to tiptoe when they sing "tippy toe."

2. Ask one or more leaders to tiptoe around the room. As the class sings "fine" and "mine" (the half notes), leader taps a seated child. Tapped child steps in line behind leader.

2. The one she's been saving,
   The one she's been saving,
   The one she's been saving
   to make a feather bed.

3. She died in the mill pond,
   She died in the mill pond,
   She died in the mill pond
   standing on her head.

4. The goslings are crying,
   The goslings are crying,
   The goslings are crying
   because the goose is dead.

Bluebird through My Window

Georgia

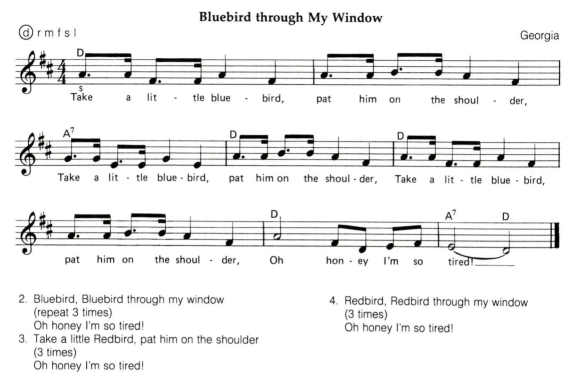

2. Bluebird, Bluebird through my window
   (repeat 3 times)
   Oh honey I'm so tired!
3. Take a little Redbird, pat him on the shoulder
   (3 times)
   Oh honey I'm so tired!
4. Redbird, Redbird through my window
   (3 times)
   Oh honey I'm so tired!

Transcribed from Archive of Folk Song Recording AFS 311, Library of Congress, Washington, D.C.

Formation   Single circle. One player is the "bluebird."

Action   *Verse One:* Bluebird selects a player and taps shoulders. Tapped player is new bluebird.
Verse Two: Players join hands and raise arms to form arches. Bluebird weaves through "windows."

Eencie Weencie Spider

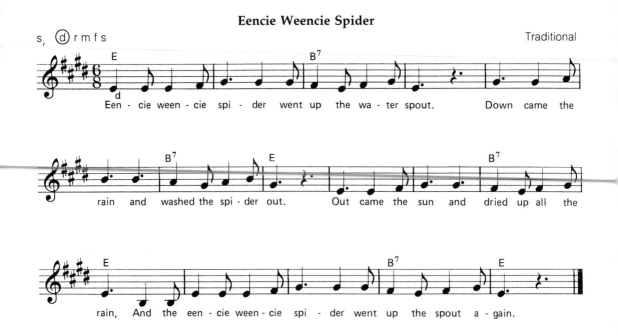

Traditional

s, (d) r m f s

Een - cie ween - cie spi - der went up the wa - ter spout. Down came the
rain and washed the spi - der out. Out came the sun and dried up all the
rain, And the een - cie ween - cie spi - der went up the spout a - gain.

Finger Play

Phrase one — Palms face outward. Wiggle fingers and move hands upward.

Phrase two — Stretch fingers outward. Wiggle fingers and move hands down.

Phrase three — Form large circle with arms and move circle from side to side.

Phrase four — Repeat action of phrase one.

If You're Happy

s, l, t, (d) r m f

Traditional

If you're hap-py and you know it, clap your hands! (clap, clap) If you're

hap-py and you know it, clap your hands! (clap, clap) If you're

hap-py and you know it, then your face will sure-ly show it, If you're

hap-py and you know it, clap your hands! (clap, clap)

2. If you're happy and you know it, stamp your feet!
   (stamp, stamp)
3. If you're happy and you know it, shout hooray!
   (Hoo-ray!)

4. If you're happy and you know it, do all three!

Draw a Bucket of Water

s, l, t, (d) r m f s

Mississippi

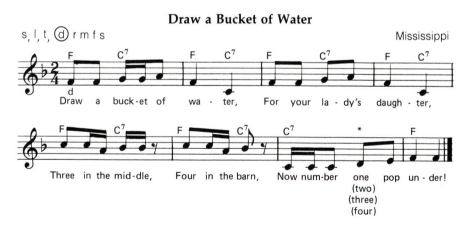

Draw a buck-et of wa-ter, For your la-dy's daugh-ter,

Three in the mid-dle, Four in the barn, Now num-ber one pop un-der!
(two)
(three)
(four)

Transcribed from Archive of Folk Song Recording AFS 3052, Library of Congress, Washington, D.C.

Formation	Children in groups of four. Numbers 1 and 2 face each other and hold hands; 3 and 4 reach over and across the arms of 1 and 2.

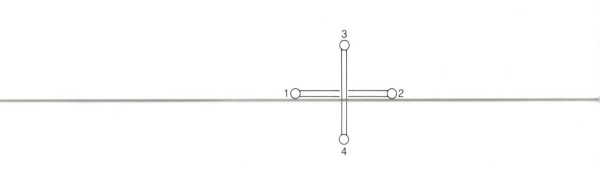

Action	Players place one foot in front of the other and, on the beat, rock back and forth in a push–pull motion.
	Verse One: At the * player number 1 "pops" to the center under the arms of 3 and 4.
	Verse Two: Player number 2 pops to the center.
	Verse Three: Player number 3 pops to the center.
	Verse Four: Player number 4 pops to the center.
	When the basket formation is complete, the tempo is doubled, and players sing the song once more. The group jumps together on the beat and rotates in a clockwise direction.

On a Mountain Stands a Lady

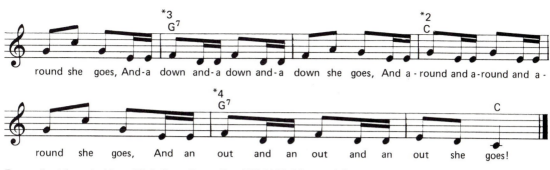

round she goes, And-a down and-a down and-a down she goes, And a - round and a-round and a -

round she goes, And an out and an out and an out she goes!

Transcribed from Archive of Folk Song Recording AFS 3650, Library of Congress, Washington, D.C.

Formation   Line. Two players turn the rope.

Action   Players follow in succession and perform the following
              actions:
              *1 jump in
              *2 turn around
              *3 squat down
              *4 jump out

Are You Sleeping

s, ⓓ r m f s l   Traditional round

Are   you sleep - ing,   are   you sleep - ing,   Broth - er   John,   Broth - er   John?

Morn-ing bells are ring - ing,   morn-ing bells are ring - ing,   ding dong ding!   Ding dong ding!

When children are familiar with this song, divide the group into four parts
and sing "Are You Sleeping" as a round.

Miss Lucy

Transcribed from the singing of Mary McGaffee. Remembered from childhood in Oak Harbor, Washington.

Formation   Players facing partners, holding hands across.

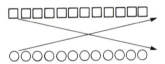

Action   *Verse One:* All players perform movements as indicated above text.

R—bend left knee, angle right foot outward at 45-degree angle, and place right heel on floor in front of body.

L—bend right knee, angle left foot outward at 45-degree angle, and place left heel on floor in front of body.

Verse Two: Players drop hands and take four steps backward, clapping on the offbeat. Player O improvises a movement (walk, jump, skip, etc.) to the end of the opposite line.

Verse Three: Player X imitates action of player O, moving to the end of the opposite line. On "All the way home," players move forward and clasp hands with original partner. Game begins again with new players at head of lines.

Scotland's Burning

When you know this song well, sing it as a four-part round. Play the following chord pattern throughout the song:

Ten in the Bed

Sing "Ten in the Bed" ten times, decreasing the number with each repetition. Conclude the song by singing:

Adam Had Seven Sons

s, l, (d) r m f s l

Mississippi

d
Ad-am had sev-en sons, Sev-en sons had Ad - am, And they all were bright and gay
(well and fed)

and they did what Ad-am said, Let's all do this, let's all do this said Ad - am!

Transcribed from Archive of Folk Song Recording AFS 884, Library of Congress, Washington, D.C.

Formation   Standing, arm's length apart.

Action   Song is repeated five times. Each time the song is sung, a new motion is added at the *. Motions continue throughout.

First motion: On the first beat of each measure, right arm is raised to the side and over head.

Second motion: Left arm is raised to the side and over head.

Third motion: Right foot is extended to the right side.

Fourth motion: Left foot is extended to the left side. Players are now performing the traditional jumping-jack movement.

Johnny, Are You Ready?

s, l, t, (d) m s

Louisiana

m
John-ny, Hey Hey! Are you read-y? Hey Hey! Go - ing to the ball - room Sat-ur-day

spoken

night, Gon - na dance all night, this Sat - ur - day night, Let's get on board!

Transcribed from Archive of Folk Song Recording AFS 614, Library of Congress, Washington, D.C.

Michael Finnegan

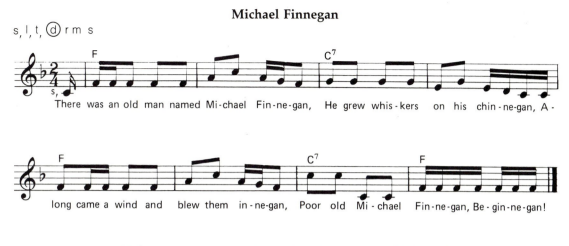

s, l, t, ⓓ r m s

There was an old man named Mi-chael Fin-ne-gan, He grew whis-kers on his chin-ne-gan, A-
long came a wind and blew them in-ne-gan, Poor old Mi-chael Fin-ne-gan, Be-gin-ne-gan!

Make up new verses about the adventures of Michael Finnegan.

Kum Bah Yah

ⓓ r m f s l

Some-one's cry - ing Lord, Kum bah yah, Some-one's cry - ing Lord, Kum bah yah, Some-one's
hap - py   hap - py

cry - ing Lord, Kum bah yah, Oh Lord,— Kum bah yah.
hap - py

Add the following formal signs (sign language) as you sing "Kum Bah Yah."

Some: Draw right hand (little finger side) across left palm.

One's: Point index finger upward.

Crying: Draw imaginary tears down side of face.

Happy: Move hand in an upward and outward motion twice.

Lord: Move hand across chest from left shoulder to right side of wrist.

Kum bah: Independently rotate hands in a circular motion toward body.

Yah: With palms up, move hands in a circular motion.

Oh: Shape hand in an *O*. Move hand to right and lift index and middle fingers.

Mary Had a Baby

s, l, (d) r m s l

Ma-ry had a ba-by, Yes, Lord, Ma-ry had a ba-by, Yes, my Lord, Ma-ry had a ba-by, Yes, Lord, The peo-ple keep a-com-in' an' the train done gone.

2. What did they name Him? (repeat three times)
3. Named Him Je-sus.
4. Where did they lay Him?
5. Laid Him in a man-ger.

Don Gato

Folk song from Mexico

① t, d d ir m f s
English words by Margaret Marks

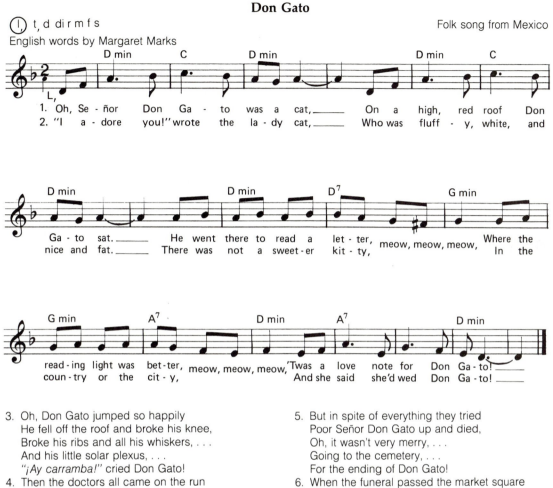

1. Oh, Se - ñor Don Ga - to was a cat,_____ On a high, red roof Don
2. "I a - dore you!" wrote the la - dy cat,_____ Who was fluff - y, white, and

Ga - to sat._____ He went there to read a let - ter, meow, meow, meow, Where the
nice and fat._____ There was not a sweet - er kit - ty, In the

read - ing light was bet - ter, meow, meow, meow, 'Twas a love note for Don Ga - to!_____
coun - try or the cit - y, And she said she'd wed Don Ga - to!_____

3. Oh, Don Gato jumped so happily
   He fell off the roof and broke his knee,
   Broke his ribs and all his whiskers, . . .
   And his little solar plexus, . . .
   "¡Ay carramba!" cried Don Gato!
4. Then the doctors all came on the run
   Just to see if something could be done,
   And they held a consultation, . . .
   About how to save their patient, . . .
   How to save Señor Don Gato!

5. But in spite of everything they tried
   Poor Señor Don Gato up and died,
   Oh, it wasn't very merry, . . .
   Going to the cemetery, . . .
   For the ending of Don Gato!
6. When the funeral passed the market square
   Such a smell of fish was in the air,
   Though his burial was slated, . . .
   He became re-animated! . . .
   He came back to life, Don Gato!

Grandpa's Whiskers

s, l, t, ⓓ r m

Traditional

Verse G

1. We have a dear old grand-pa, We see him ev-'ry day, He

D⁷   G

has a set of whisk-ers ___ that are al-ways in the way.

Refrain   A

Oh, they're al-ways in the way, The cows eat them for hay, They

D⁷   G

hide the dirt on fa-ther's shirt, They're al-ways in the way!

2. Each night we meet for dinner, We make a
   happy group,
   Until dear grandpa's whiskers get tangled in the
   soup.
3. Now grandma has a habit of chewing in her
   sleep,
   She chews on grandpa's whiskers, She thinks
   they're shredded wheat!

4. When grandpa goes out swimming, no swimming suit for him,
   He wraps his whiskers 'round him and then he
   plunges in!

My Hat

Decide on appropriate motions for the starred words. Sing the song as written. Each time the song is repeated, eliminate a word and substitute the motion.

I Love the Mountains

Traditional camp song

1. Practice the following chord sequence on the piano or a strumming instrument. Use this sequence as an accompaniment for "I Love the Mountains."

2. Sing this song as a three-part round. Add chordal accompaniment.

Get on Board

Spiritual

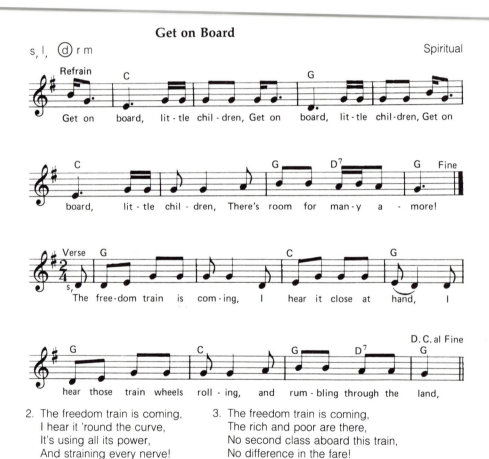

2. The freedom train is coming,
   I hear it 'round the curve,
   It's using all its power,
   And straining every nerve!

3. The freedom train is coming,
   The rich and poor are there,
   No second class aboard this train,
   No difference in the fare!

Swing Low, Sweet Chariot

s,l, (d) r m s l

The refrains of ''Swing Low, Sweet Chariot'' and ''All Night, All Day'' can be sung together as partner songs.

All Night, All Day

Refrain

All night, all_____ day, An - gels watch-ing o - ver me, my Lord. ___

All night, all_____ day, An - gels watch-ing o - ver me. _____ Fine

Verse

1. Now I lay me down to sleep, An - gels watch-ing o - ver me, my Lord,__
2. If I die be - fore__ I wake, An - gels watch-ing o - ver me, my Lord,__

Pray the Lord my soul__ to keep. An - gels watch-ing o - ver me. _____
Pray the Lord my soul__ to take. An - gels watch-ing o - ver me. _____ D. C. al Fine

Pretty Saro

U.S.

Way down in the val - ley in a lone - some place, I pine for the

smile on my lit - tle girl's face. Fare - well, pret - ty Sa - ro, I bid you a -

dieu; As I dream of pret - ty Sa - ro, wher - ev - er I go.

Worried Man Blues

It takes a wor-ried man to sing a wor-ried song, It takes a wor-ried man to sing a wor-ried song, It takes a wor-ried man to sing a wor-ried song, i'm wor-ried now but I won't be wor-ried long.

I Saw Three Ships

England
Descant by Phyllis Irwin

Sail - ing, sail - ing, sail - ing on Chris - si - mas.

In the morn - ing, Chris - si - mas Day, Chris - si - mas Day.

saw three ships come sail - ing by, On Chris - si - mas Day, on Chris - si - mas Day. I

In the morn - ing Chris - si - mas Day in the morn - ing.

saw three ships come sail - ing by, on Chris - si - mas Day in the morn - ing.

2. And what was in those ships all three,
   On Chrissimas Day, on Chrissimas Day?
   And what was in those ships all three,
   On Chrissimas Day in the morning?

3. Inside those ships were Wise Men three,
   On Chrissimas Day, on Chrissimas Day.
   Inside those ships were Wise Men three,
   On Chrissimas Day in the morning.

Cockles and Mussels

Irish folk song

From *The Music Book*, Level 6. Copyright 1981 by Holt, Rinehart & Winston, Publishers. Reprinted by permission.

Tell Me Why

s, l, t, ⓓ r m f

Traditional

Descant

1. Tell ___ me why ___ the stars do shine, Tell ___ me why ___ the i - vy twines,
2. Be-cause God made ___ the stars to shine, Be-cause God made ___ the i - vy twine,

Melody

Tell ___ me why ___ the sky's so blue, And I will tell you just why I love you.
Be-cause God made ___ the sky so blue, Be-cause God made you, that's why I love you.

"Tell Me Why" is a traditional camp song. Divide the class in half and sing both parts together!

Hey Ho, Nobody Home!

m, s, ⓛ t, d r m

Em Bm ②Em Bm Em Bm ③Em Bm Em Bm

Hey ho, no-bod-y home, Meat nor drink nor mon-ey do I own, Still I will be mer - ry ver-y mer-ry.

Try this song as a three-part round.

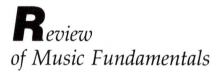

APPENDIX A

*R*eview
of Music Fundamentals

Music is written on five parallel lines called a *staff*.

Clef signs are used to assign names to the lines and spaces. The *G-Clef*, or *Treble Clef*, assigns the letter G to the second line of the staff.

When G is in the second line, notes in the remaining lines and spaces are assigned as follows:

Ledger lines are used to extend a melody above or below the staff.

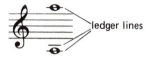

The *F-Clef*, or *Bass Clef*, assigns the name *F* to the fourth line of the staff.

Whole and Half Steps

The piano keyboard is composed of a sequence of black and white keys. The distance between any key and its nearest neighbor, an adjacent key (black or white), is called a *half step*. A *whole step* consists of two half steps.

Piano keyboard

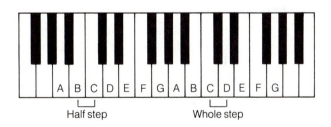

Sharps and Flats

The flat sign (♭) lowers the pitch of a given note by a half step. In music notation, the flat sign traditionally precedes the altered note.

In conversation, the note name is pronounced first. The note in the above example is referred to as *B flat*. The sharp sign (♯) raises the pitch of a given note by a half step.

The natural sign (♮) cancels, in effect, a flat or a sharp. In the following example, G sharp is followed by G, or G natural.

Scales

Notes can be arranged in a stepwise sequence, or "row." This arrangement is referred to as a *scale*. The first note of a scale is the home tone, or tone center. The tone center in the following example is C.

This is the C major scale. Major scales can be constructed using any note as the tone center. The arrangement of whole and half steps, however, remains constant: W,W,H, W,W,W,H. Minor scales have the following arrangement of whole and half steps:

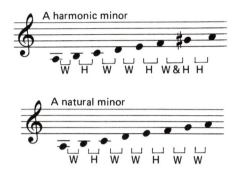

Some scales contain "gaps." One such scale is the *pentatonic scale.*

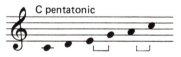

Key Signature

Scales can be constructed using any tone or note as the home tone or tone center. Sharps or flats are added, as necessary, to maintain the required sequence of whole and half steps.

Traditionally, the required sharps or flats are placed at the beginning of each staff of music. This pattern of sharps or flats is called the *key signature*. Key signatures for the major and minor scales are as follows:

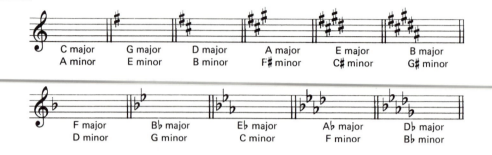

Chords

A chord is composed of three or more tones sounding simultaneously. The following chart includes the common chords associated with major and minor scales or keys.

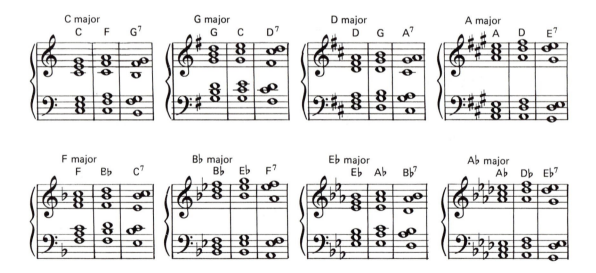

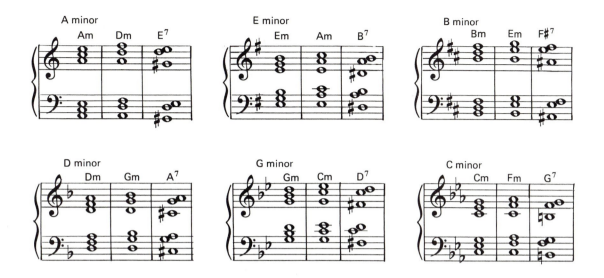

Meter

Steady beats, or pulses, in music can be grouped in twos, threes, or combinations thereof. The organization of beats in groups is called *meter*. The first beat in each group is perceived as an accented or strong beat. A sound that is one beat in length can be represented by symbols in music. One symbol that is frequently used to represent "one sound per beat" is the quarter note (♩). *Bar* lines, or *measure* lines, are used to divide beats into groups. Each group of beats is called a measure. *Double bar lines* signal the end of a composition (or section of a composition).

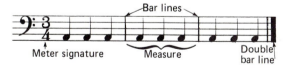

The *meter signature,* or time signature, at the beginning of a composition indicates the number of beats in a measure and the type of note that equals one beat.

Meter signature

2 ←—Two beats per measure
4 ←—Quarter note equals one beat

6 ←—Six beats per measure
8 ←—Eighth note equals one beat

Note Values

Ties enable composers to extend the value, or duration, of sounds. The following notations are equal in duration:

Tie

Dots extend the duration of a note by one half of its original value.

Dots

The following two charts show relative note values. The first chart is based on the quarter note being equal to one beat. The second chart is based on the eighth note being equal to one beat.

Symbol	Name	Duration	Rhythm syllables
♩	Quarter note	1 beat	Ta
♫	Eighth notes	1 beat (½ beat each)	Ti-ti
♪	Eighth note	½ beat	Ti
𝄽	Quarter rest	1 beat	Sh
♩	Half note	2 beats	Too or Ta -
𝅝	Whole note	4 beats	Toe or ta - - -
♩.	Dotted quarter	1½ beats	Tum
♬♬	Sixteenths	1 beat (¼ each)	Ti-ri-ti-ri or Ti-ka-ti-ka
♫♬	Eighth and sixteenths	1 beat	Ti - ti-ri Ti - ti-ka
♬♫	Sixteenths and eighth	1 beat	Ti-ri-ti Ti-ka-ti
♪.♬	Dotted eighth and sixteenth	1 beat	Tim- ka
♬♪.	Sixteenth and dotted eighth	1 beat	Ti- kum
³♬♪	Triplet	1 beat	Tri-o-la

Symbol	Name	Duration	Rhythm syllables
♪	Eighth note	1 beat	Ti
♪	Eighth rest	1 beat	Sh
♫♪	Eighth notes	3 beats	Ti-ti-ti
♩ ♪	Quarter and eighth	3 beats	Ta- ti
♩.	Dotted quarter	3 beats	Tum
♩.	Dotted half	6 beats	Too
♬	Sixteenths	1 beat (½ beat each)	Ti-ka
♩. ♬	Dotted eighth, sixteenth, eighth	3 beats	Tim- ka-ti
♬ ♩.	Sixteenth, dotted eighth, eighth	3 beats	Ti-kum- ti

APPENDIX B

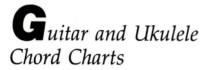

Guitar and Ukulele
Chord Charts

GUITAR CHORDS

O = open string
x = string not played

tuning

E A D G B E

C major

G major

G⁷ 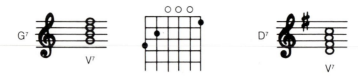 V⁷

D⁷ V⁷

F major

F  I

D major

D  I

B♭  IV

G IV

C⁷  V⁷

A⁷ 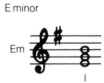 V⁷

A minor

Am I

E minor

Em I

Dm IV

Am  IV

E⁷

B⁷

D minor

Dm

G minor

Gm

Gm

Cm

A⁷

D⁷

tuning

D G B E

○ = open string

G major

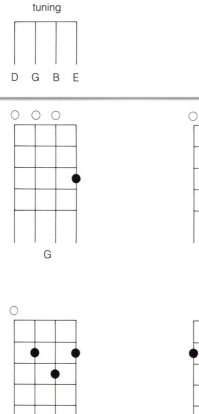

G

D⁷

C

D major

D

A⁷

G

E minor

E min

B⁷

A min

SOPRANO UKULELE CHORDS

tuning

G C E A

○ = open string

C major

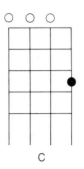

C

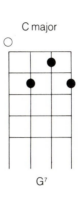

G⁷

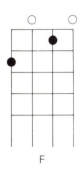

F

G major

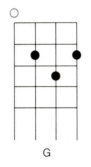

G

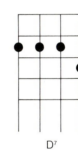

D⁷

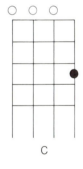

C

A minor

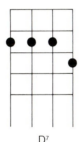

A min

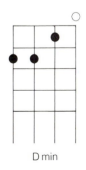

E⁷

D min

$\textbf{\textit{G}}$lossary of Musical Terms

Accidental: A symbol indicating that a pitch is to be raised a half step (♯, sharp), lowered a half step (♭, flat), or restored to the pitch within the scale (♮, natural).

Bar: A vertical line indicating measure (beat) division on a staff.

Beat: Underlying pulse in music.

Bordun: An accompaniment pattern in which two pitches, played simultaneously, are repeated over and over, creating a drone effect.

Cadence: The two chords forming the end of a section, phrase, or composition.

Chant: A short melodic idea sung over and over.

Chord: Three or more pitches sounding simultaneously.

Chromatic: Melodic movement progressing by half steps.

Coda: A short section forming an ending to a musical composition.

Descant: An independent melody used to accompany another melody.

Diatonic: A scale that includes eight pitches within an octave.

Duet: A composition featuring two performers. A performing group of two performers.

Duration: The length in time of a sound or silence.

Dynamic level: The degree of loudness or softness of a sound or sounds.

Folk songs: Songs, by unknown authors, that have been handed down from one generation to another as part of the oral tradition.

Form: The arrangement or design of musical sections, phrases, or ideas within a composition.

Fugue: A polyphonic composition in which a main melodic idea, called a subject, is stated by one voice or part and then is imitated on different pitches by one or more additional voices or parts. The overall effect is an interweaving of melodic lines that imitate and accompany each other.

Harmony: The simultaneous presence of two or more pitches.

Home tone: The first tone of a scale.

Homophony: Music in which a single melody is accompanied by a chordal harmony.

Icon: A pictorial representation of a musical sound or sequence.

Interval: The distance between two pitches.

Key: The system of pitches relating to a specific home tone.

Key signature: The sharps or flats appearing on the staff at the beginning of a composition.

Measure: The area between bar lines on a staff.

Melody: A sequential arrangement of musical tones (pitches).

Meter: Groupings of beats.

Monophony: Music in which a melody is performed without accompaniment.

Motive: A short rhythmic or melodic idea appearing several times in a musical composition.

Music: The sequential progression of organized sounds and silences.

Ostinato: A short melodic pattern sounded over and over again.

Partner songs: Two or more songs that can be sung simultaneously with pleasing effect.

Part singing: Singing in harmony.

Patsching: Patting or clapping the lap or the top of the thighs.

Percussion family: The family of instruments whose sounds are produced by a vibration of a membrane, metal or wood. They can be classified in two groups: nonpitched instruments that produce indefinite pitches and pitched instruments that produce definite pitches.

Phrase: A musical thought comparable to a sentence.

Pitch: Highness or lowness of sound.

Polyphony: Music in which two or more independent melodies are combined to create harmony.

Quartet: A musical composition featuring four performers. A performing group composed of four performers.

Rhythm: Arrangements of sounds and silences in time.

Rote song: A song that is taught by rote (through imitation).

Round: A song in which one group begins singing the melody and, upon reaching certain points, is joined by other groups, each singing the melody from the beginning.

Scale: A sequence of pitches in ascending or descending order.

Singing games: Songs accompanied by gamelike movement activities.

Staff: The five parallel lines on which music is written.

String family: All instruments in which sounds are produced by vibrating strings.

Syncopation: A rhythmic effect created by an accent or stress that does not correspond to the usual metrical accent.

Tempo: Speed of the beat.

Theme: An important musical idea within a section or composition.

Timbre: The unique quality or color of sound produced by any soundmaker.

Time signature: The numbers or symbols appearing at the beginning of a musical composition. The upper number indicates beats per measure. The lower number indicates the type of note that receives one beat.

Tone-call: Melodic fragment or motive usually with only two or three pitches. Tone-calls are often used by children in playing games, calling each other, and teasing.

Tonic chord: A chord built on the first step of a scale.

Triad: A three-note chord in which pitches are arranged at intervals of a third.

Trio: A composition featuring three performers. A performing group composed of three individuals.

Wind family: All instruments in which sounds are produced by vibrating columns of air.

Bibliography

Professional Books

Andress, Barbara L. *Music in Early Childhood.* Music Educators National Conference, 1973.

Aranoff, Frances W. *Music and Young Children,* Expanded Edition. New York: Turning Wheel Press, 1979.

Athey, Margaret and Gwen Hotchkiss. *A Galaxy of Games for the Music Class.* West Nyack: Parker, 1975.

Bayless, Kathleen M. and Marjorie S. Ramsey. *Music: A Way of Life for the Young Child,* Second Edition. Orange, Va: C. V. Mosby, 1982.

Beatty, Eleanore and Carol Schnitger. *Center In on Music: Individualized Learning Centers in the Elementary Classroom.* Champaign, Ill.: Mark Foster Music Company, 1977.

Beer, Alice S. and Mary E. Hoffman. *Teaching Music.* Morristown, N.J.: Silver Burdett Company, 1982.

Bonis, Ferenc, editor. *The Selected Writings of Zoltán Kodály.* New York: Boosey and Hawkes, 1974.

Burton, Leon and William Hughes. *Music Play— Learning Activities for Young Children.* Reading, Mass.: Addison-Wesley, 1980.

Choksy, Lois. *The Kodály Context.* Englewood Cliffs, N.J.: Prentice–Hall, 1981.

Choksy, Lois. *The Kodály Method.* Englewood Cliffs, N.J.: Prentice–Hall, 1974.

Davis, Marilyn Kornreich. *Music Dictionary.* London: Faber and Faber, Ltd., 1975.

Edwards, Eleanor M. *Music Education for the Deaf.* Merriam–Eddy, 1974.

Flavell, John H. *The Developmental Psychology of Jean Piaget.* Princeton, N.J.: D. Van Nostrand, 1963.

Gell, Heather. *Music Movement and the Young Child,* rev. ed. Hialeah, Fla.: Columbia Pictures Publications, 1973.

Gesell, Arnold and Francis Ilg. *The Child from Five to Ten.* New York: Harper & Row, 1946.

Gesell, Arnold, Francis Ilg, and Louise Bates Ames. *Youth: The Years from Ten to Sixteen.* New York: Harper & Brothers, 1956.

Graham, Richard and Alice Beer. *Teaching Music to the Exceptional Child.* Englewood Cliffs, N.J.: Prentice–Hall, 1980.

Hackett, Patricia, et al. *The Musical Classroom: Models, Skills and Backgrounds for Elementary Teaching.* Englewood Cliffs, N.J.: Prentice–Hall, 1979.

Hallahan, Daniel P. and James M. Kauffman. *Exceptional Children: Introduction to Special Education*, Second Edition. Englewood Cliffs, N.J.: Prentice–Hall, 1982.

Hardesty, Kay W. *Music for the Exceptional Child*. Palo Alto, Calif.: Silver Burdett Company, 1979.

Harrison, Lois N. *Getting Started in Elementary Music Education*. Englewood Cliffs, N.J.: Prentice–Hall, 1983.

Havighurst, Robert J. *Developmental Tasks and Education*. New York: Longmans, Green, and Company, 1953.

Havighurst, Robert J. *Human Development and Education*. New York: Longmans, Green, and Company, 1953.

Hawkinson, John and Martha Faulhaber. *Rhythms, Music, and Instruments to Make*. Chicago: Albert Whitman and Company, 1975.

Herrold, Rebecca. *New Approaches to Elementary Music Education*. Englewood Cliffs, N.J.: Prentice–Hall, 1984.

Hochheimer, Laura. *A Sequential Sourcebook for Elementary School Music: A Curriculum Guide and Sourcebook Combined*, Second Edition. St. Louis, Missouri: Magnamusic Baton, Inc., 1980.

Hotchkiss, Gwen and Margaret Athey. *Treasures of Individualized Activities for the Music Class*. West Nyack: Parker, 1977.

Joyce, Mary. *First Steps in Teaching Creative Dance*. Palo Alto, Calif.: Mayfield, 1973.

Keetman, Gunild. *Elementaria, First Acquaintance with Orff-Schulwerk*. Totowa, N.J.: European–American Music, 1974.

Keller, Wilhelm. *Introduction to Music for Children*. Totowa, N.J.: European–American Music, 1974.

Landis, Beth and Polly Carder. *Eclectic Curriculum in American Music Education: Contribution of Dalcroze, Kodály and Orff*. Reston, Va.: Music Educators National Conference, 1972.

List, Lynne K. *Music, Art and Drama Activities for the Elementary Classroom*. New York: Teachers College Press, 1982.

Nash, Grace. *Creative Approaches to Child Development with Music, Languages, and Movement*. Sherman Oaks, Calif.: Alfred Publishing Company, 1974.

Nocera, Sona D. *Reaching the Special Student through Music*. Morristown, N.J.: Silver Burdett Company, 1979.

Nye, Vernice T. *Music for Young Children*, Third Edition. Dubuque, Iowa: Wm. C. Brown, 1983.

O'Brien, James P. *Teaching Music*. New York: Holt, Rinehart & Winston, 1983.

Piaget, Jean. *The Child's Conception of Movement and Speed*. London: Rutledge and Kegan Paul, 1970.

Piaget, Jean. *The Child's Conception of Number*. New York: W. W. Norton, 1965.

Piaget, Jean. *Psychology of Intelligence*. Totowa, N.J.: Littlefield, Adams, 1968.

Pratt, Rosalie, editor. *Music Education for the Handicapped: Second International Symposium*. Bloomington, Ind.: T.I.S., 1983.

Pratt, Rosalie Rebello and Meg Patterson. *Elementary Music for All Learners*. Sherman Oaks, Calif.: Alfred Publishing Company, 1981.

Raebeck, Lois and Lawrence Wheeler. *New Approaches to Music in the Elementary School*, Fourth Edition. Dubuque, Iowa: Wm. C. Brown, 1980.

Swanson, Bessie. *Music in the Education of Children*, Fourth Edition. Belmont, Calif.: Wadsworth, 1981.

Swanson, Leland C. *Theories of Learning: Traditional Perspectives/Contemporary Developments*. Belmont, Calif.: Wadsworth, 1980.

Szonyi, Erzsebet. *Kodály's Principles in Practice*. New York: Boosey and Hawkes, 1973.

Vernazza, Marcelle. *Music Plus: For the Young Child in Special Education*. Boulder, Colo.: Pruett, 1978.

Wheeler, Lawrence and Lois Raebeck. *Orff and Kodály Adapted for the Elementary School*, Second Edition. Dubuque, Iowa: Wm. C. Brown, 1977.

Winslow, Robert and Leon Dallin. *Music Skills for Classroom Teachers*, Sixth Edition. Dubuque, Iowa: Wm. C. Brown, 1984.

Wiseman, Ann. *Making Musical Things*. New York: Charles Scribners and Sons, 1979.

Zernke, Lorna and Katinka S. Daniel. *Kodály Thirty-Five Lesson Plans and Folk Song Supplement*, Second Edition. Champaign, Ill.: Mark Foster Music Company, 1976.

Series Texts

American Book Company, 150 West 50th Street, New York, New York, 10020. *New Dimensions in Music* Series, Robert Choate et al., 1979.

Holt and Winston, Inc., 383 Madison Avenue, New York, New York, 10017. *The Music Book* Series, Eunice Boardman and Barbara Andress, 1981.

The Macmillan Company, Inc., 200 E. Brown Street, Riverside, New Jersey, 08075. *Macmillan Music* Series, Mary Val Marsh et al., 1983.

Silver Burdett Company, 250 James Street, Morristown, New Jersey, 07960. *Silver Burdett MUSIC* Series, Elizabeth Crook et al., 1981.

Recordings

Bailey, Charity. *More Music Time and Stories.* Folkways Records.

Bailey, Charity. *Music Time with Charity Bailey.* Folkways Records.

Gillespie, Avon. *In Workshop.* Belwin/Mills Publishing Company.

Glazer, Tom and the Do Re Mi Children's Chorus. *On Top of Spaghetti.* MCA Records, Inc.

Jenkins, Ella. *Play Your Instruments and Make a Pretty Sound.* Folkways Records.

Richman, Trudie. *Songs of Work and Play.* Folkways Records.

Schwartz, Tony. *Sound Effects.* Folkways Records.

Seeger, Pete. *American Game and Activity Songs for Children.* Folkways Records.

Seeger, Pete. *Birds, Beasts, Bugs and Little Fishes.* Folkways Records.

Seeger, Pete and Erik Darling. *Camp Songs.* Scholastic Records.

Smith, Charles Edward, editor. *Music Down Home: An Introduction to Negro Folk Music, U.S.A.* Folkways Records.

Wood, Lucille. *The Small Listener.* Bowmar Records.

Wood, Lucille, editor. *The Small Singer* (Volumes 1 and 2). Bowmar Records.

Adventures in Sound. Melody House.

The Lives and Music of Bach, Beethoven, Chopin and Mozart. Sine Qua Non Cassettes and Records.

Sing Children Sing: Songs of the Congo. Caedmon Records.

Story of the Nutcracker. Caedmon Records.

Song and Activity Collections

Adler, Marvin S. and Jesse C. McCarroll. *Making Music Fun: A Complete Collection of Games, Puzzles and Activities for the Elementary Classroom.* Englewood Cliffs, N.J.: Prentice–Hall, 1981.

Beall, Pamela and Susan Nipp. *Wee Sing and Play: Musical Games and Rhymes for Children.* Los Angeles: Price, Stern and Sloan, 1983.

Beall, Pamela and Susan Nipp. *Wee Sing: Children's Songs and Fingerplays.* Los Angeles: Price, Stern and Sloan, 1980.

Chase, Richard. *American Folk Tales and Songs.* New York: Dover, 1971.

Dallin, Leon and Lynn Dallin. *Folk Songster.* Dubuque, Iowa: Wm. C. Brown, 1967.

Erdei, Peter. *150 American Folk Songs to Sing, Read and Play.* New York: Boosey and Hawkes, 1974.

Fowke, Edith. *Sally Go Round the Sun.* New York: Doubleday, 1969.

Frazee, Jane. *Singing in the Season.* St. Louis: Magnamusic-Baton, Inc., 1983.

Fulton, Eleanor and Pat Smith. *Let's Slice the Ice: Black Children's Ring Games and Chants.* St. Louis, Missouri: Magnamusic, 1978.

Glazer, Tom. *Do Your Ears Hang Low? Fifty More Musical Fingerplays.* New York: Doubleday, 1980.

Glazer, Tom. *Eye Winker, Tom Tinker, Chin Chopper.* New York: Doubleday, 1973.

Hart, Jane. *Singing Bee! A Collection of Favorite Children's Songs.* New York: William Morrow, 1982.

Johnson, Laura. *Simplified Lummi Stick Activities.* Long Beach, N.J.: Kimbo Educational, 1976.

Jones, Bessie and Bess Hawes. *Step It Down.* New York: Harper & Row, 1972.

Komlos, Katalina et al. *One Hundred and Fifty American Folk Songs to Sing and Play.* New York: Boosey and Hawkes, 1974.

Landeck, Beatrice and Elizabeth Crook. *Wake Up and Sing*. New York: Edward B. Marks, 1969.

Langstaff, John and Carol Langstaff. *Shimmy Shimmy Coke-Ca-Pop!* New York: Doubleday, 1973.

Langstaff, John and Nancy Langstaff. *Jim Along, Josie*. New York: Harcourt Brace Jovanovich, 1970.

Larrick, Nancy. *The Wheels of the Bus Go Round and Round*. San Carlos, Calif.: Golden Gate Junior Books, 1972.

Lomax, Alan. *The Folk Songs of North America*. New York: Doubleday, 1975.

Nelson, Esther L. *The Funny Song Book*. New York: Sterling Publishing Company, 1984.

Nelson, Esther L. *Musical Games for Children of All Ages*. New York: Sterling Publishing Company, 1976.

Nelson, Esther L. *The Silly Song Book*. New York: Sterling Publishing Company, 1981.

Palmer, Hap. *Hap Palmer Favorites*. Sherman Oaks, Calif.: Lathrop, Lee and Shepard Company, 1977.

Quackenbush, Robert. *The Holiday Songbook*. New York: Lathrop, Lee and Shepard Company, 1977.

Shotwell, Rita, et al. *Musical Games, Fingerplays and Rhythmic Activities for Early Childhood*. New York: Parker, 1983.

Terri, Salli. *Round America*. New York: Lawson Gould Music Publishers, 1976.

Terri, Salli. *Rounds for Everyone from Everywhere*. New York: Lawson Gould Music Publishers, 1966.

Yolen, Jane. *Rounds about Rounds*. New York: Franklin Watts, 1977.

Winn, Marie. *The Fireside Book of Children's Songs*. New York: Simon & Schuster, 1966.

Basic Listening Series

Adventures in Music, A New Record Library for Elementary Schools, RCA Victor Recording Corporation. (Le = long play, Les = stereo.) A teacher's guide is included in the folder for each album. (See alphabetical listing of music by composers on the following pages.)

Grade 1, Volume 1 (Le/Les 1000)
Grade 1, Volume 2 (Le/Les 1010)
Grade 2, Volume 1 (Le/Les 1001)
Grade 2, Volume 2 (Le/Les 1011)
Grade 3, Volume 1 (Le/Les 1002)
Grade 3, Volume 2 (Le/Les 1003)
Grade 4, Volume 1 (Le/Les 1004)
Grade 4, Volume 2 (Le/Les 1005)
Grade 5, Volume 1 (Le/Les 1006)
Grade 5, Volume 2 (Le/Les 1007)
Grade 6, Volume 1 (Le/Les 1008)
Grade 6, Volume 2 (Le/Les 1009)

Bowmar Orchestral Library, Bowmar Educational Records. Organized by topics, each album is accompanied by wall charts of themes and suggestions for the teacher. (See alphabetical listing of music by composers on the following pages.)

BOL #51 ANIMALS AND CIRCUS
BOL #52 NATURE AND MAKE-BELIEVE
BOL #53 PICTURES AND PATTERNS
BOL #54 MARCHES
BOL #55 DANCES, PART I
BOL #56 DANCES, PART II
BOL #57 FAIRY TALES IN MUSIC
BOL #58 STORIES IN BALLET AND OPERA
BOL #59 LEGENDS IN MUSIC
BOL #60 UNDER MANY FLAGS
BOL #61 AMERICAN SCENES
BOL #62 MASTERS IN MUSIC
BOL #63 CONCERT MATINEE
BOL #64 MINIATURES IN MUSIC
BOL #65 MUSIC, USA
BOL #66 ORIENTAL SCENES
BOL #67 FANTASY IN MUSIC
BOL #68 CLASSROOM CONCERT
BOL #69 MUSIC OF THE DANCE: STRAVINSKY
BOL #70 MUSIC OF THE SEA AND SKY
BOL #71 SYMPHONIC MOVEMENTS, NO. 1
BOL #72 SYMPHONIC MOVEMENTS, NO. 2
BOL #73 SYMPHONIC STYLES
BOL #74 TWENTIETH CENTURY AMERICA

BOL #75 U.S. HISTORY IN MUSIC
BOL #76 OVERTURES
BOL #77 SCHEHEREZADE
BOL #78 MUSICAL KALEIDOSCOPE
BOL #79 MUSIC OF THE DRAMA:
   WAGNER
BOL #80 PETROUCHKA
BOL #81 ROGUES IN MUSIC
BOL #82 MUSIC IN PICTURES
BOL #83 ENSEMBLES, LARGE AND
   SMALL

Adventures in Music Contents

Anderson: *Irish Suite—The Girl I Left Behind Me,* Gr. 5, Vol. 2

Arnold: *English Suite—Grazioso* (7th movement), Gr. 1, Vol. 2
   English Suite—Allegro Non Troppo (5th movement), Gr. 2, Vol. 2

Bach: *Cantata 147—Jesu, Joy of Man's Desiring,* Gr. 5, Vol. 1
   Little Fugue in G Minor (arr. by L. Cailliet), Gr. 6, Vol. 1
   Suite No. 2—Badinerie, Gr. 3, Vol. 1
   Suite No. 2—Rondeau, Gr. 2, Vol. 2
   Suite No. 2—Gigue, Gr. 1, Vol. 1

Bartók: *Hungarian Sketches—Bear Dance,* Gr. 3, Vol. 2
   Hungarian Sketches—Evening in the Village, Gr. 5, Vol. 2
   Mikrokosmos Suite No. 2—Jack-in-the-Box, Gr. 2, Vol. 1
   Mikrokosmos—Diary of a Fly (Moto perpetuo, No. 142), Gr. 1, Vol. 2

Beethoven: *Symphony No. 8—Second Movement,* Gr. 6, Vol. 1

Berlioz: *The Damnation of Faust—Ballet of the Sylphs,* Gr. 1, Vol. 1

Bizet: *L'Arlesienne Suite No. 1—Minuetto,* Gr. 4, Vol. 2
   L'Arlesienne Suite No. 2—Farandole, Gr. 6, Vol. 1
   Carmen—Changing of the Guard, Gr. 3, Vol. 2
   Carmen Suite—Dragoons of Alcala, Gr. 2, Vol. 2
   Children's Games—The Ball; Cradle Song; Leap Frog, Gr. 1, Vol. 1

Borodin: *In the Steppes of Central Asia,* Gr. 6, Vol. 1

Brahms: *Hungarian Dance No. 1,* Gr. 5, Vol. 2

Cailliet: *Pop! Goes the Weasel—Variations,* Gr. 4, Vol. 1

Carpenter: *Adventures in a Perambulator—The Hurdy-Gurdy,* Gr. 5, Vol. 2

Chabrier: *España Rapsodie,* Gr. 5, Vol. 1
   Marche Joyeuse, Gr. 4, Vol. 1

Charpentier: *Impressions of Italy—On Muleback,* Gr. 5, Vol. 1

Cimarosa: *Cimarosiana—Non Troppo Mosso* (3rd movement), Gr. 2, Vol. 2

Coates: *London Suite—Knightsbridge March,* Gr. 5, Vol. 2

Copland: *Billy the Kid Ballet Suite—Street in a Frontier Town,* Gr. 6, Vol. 1
   The Red Pony Suite—Circus Music, Gr. 3, Vol. 1
   The Red Pony Suite—Dream March, Gr. 2, Vol. 2
   Rodeo—Hoe-Down, Gr. 5, Vol. 2

Corelli-Pinelli: *Suite for Strings—Sarabande,* Gr. 6, Vol. 2

Debussy: *Children's Corner Suite—The Snow Is Dancing,* Gr. 3, Vol. 1
   La Mer—Play of the Waves, Gr. 6, Vol. 2

Delibes: *Coppélia—Waltz of the Doll,* Gr. 1, Vol. 1
   Coppélia—Swanhilde's Waltz, Gr. 2, Vol. 2
   The King Is Amused—Lesquercarde, Gr. 1, Vol. 2

Dvořák: *Slavonic Dance No. 7,* Gr. 4, Vol. 2

Elgar: *Wand of Youth Suite No. 1—Fairies and Giants,* Gr. 3, Vol. 1
   Wand of Youth Suite No. 2—Fountain Dance, Gr. 2, Vol. 1
   Wand of Youth Suite—Sun Dance, Gr. 2, Vol. 2

Falla: *La Vida Breve—Spanish Dance No. 1,* Gr. 6, Vol. 1

Fauré: *Dolly—Berceuse,* Gr. 2, Vol. 1

German: *Henry VIII Suite—Morris Dance,* Gr. 1, Vol. 2

Ginastera: *Estancia—Wheat Dance,* Gr. 4, Vol. 1

Glière: *The Red Poppy—Russian Sailors' Dance,* Gr. 6, Vol. 2

Gluck: *Armide Ballet Suite—Musette,* Gr. 2, Vol. 2
   Iphigenie in Aulis—Air Gai, Gr. 1, Vol. 1

Gottschalk-Kay: *Cakewalk Ballet Suite—Grand Walkaround,* Gr. 5, Vol. 1

Gould: *American Salute,* Gr. 5, Vol. 1

Gounod: *Faust Ballet Suite—Waltz No. 1*, Gr. 3, Vol. 1

Grainger: *Londonderry Air*, Gr. 4, Vol. 2

Grétry: *Céphale et Procris—Gigue* (arr. by Mottl), Gr. 1, Vol. 1

Céphale et Procris—Tambourin (arr. by Mottl), Gr. 2, Vol. 1

Grieg: *Lyric Suite—Norwegian Rustic March*, Gr. 4, Vol. 1

Peer Gynt Suite—Anitra's Dance, Gr. 1, Vol. 2

Peer Gynt Suite—In the Hall of the Mountain King, Gr. 3, Vol. 2

Griffes: *The White Peacock*, Gr. 6, Vol. 1

Grofé: *Death Valley Suite—Desert Water Hole*, Gr. 4, Vol. 1

Guarnieri: *Brazilian Dance*, Gr. 6, Vol. 2

Handel: *Royal Fireworks Music—Bourrée, Menuetto No. 2*, Gr. 3, Vol. 2

Water Music—Hornpipe, Gr. 2, Vol. 1

Hanson: *For the First Time—Bells*, Gr. 1, Vol. 2

Merry Mount Suite—Children's Dance, Gr. 3, Vol. 1

Herbert: *Babes in Toyland—March of the Toys*, Gr. 2, Vol. 1

Natoma—Dagger Dance, Gr. 3, Vol. 1

Holst: *The Perfect Fool—Spirits of the Earth*, Gr. 6, Vol. 2

Howe: *Sand*, Gr. 2, Vol. 2

Humperdinck: *Hänsel and Gretel—Prelude*, Gr. 5, Vol. 2

Ibert: *Divertissement—Parade*, Gr. 1, Vol. 1

Histoires No. 2—The Little White Donkey, Gr. 2, Vol. 1

Kabalevsky: *The Comedians—March and Comedians' Galop*, Gr. 3, Vol. 1

The Comedians—Pantomime, Gr. 1, Vol. 1

The Comedians—Waltz, Gr. 1, Vol. 2

Khachaturian: *Gayne—Dance of the Rose Maidens*, Gr. 1, Vol. 2

Masquerade Suite—Waltz, Gr. 4, Vol. 2

Kodály: *Háry János Suite—Entrance of the Emperor and His Court*, Gr. 4, Vol. 2

Háry János Suite—Viennese Musical Clock, Gr. 2, Vol. 1

Lecuona: *Suite Andalucia—Andalucia*, Gr. 4, Vol. 1

Liadov: *Eight Russian Folk Songs—Berceuse*, Gr. 1, Vol. 2

Lully: *Ballet Suite—March*, Gr. 3, Vol. 2

McBride: *Pumpkin-Eater's Little Fugue*, Gr. 2, Vol. 2

Punch and the Judy—Pony Express, Gr. 1, Vol. 2

McDonald: *Children's Symphony—Allegro*, Gr. 3, Vol. 2

Children's Symphony (3rd movement)—*Farmer in the Dell, Jingle Bells*, Gr. 2, Vol. 1

MacDowell: *Second* (Indian) *Suite—In Wartime*, Gr. 5, Vol. 1

Massenet: *Le Cid—Aragonaise*, Gr. 1, Vol. 1

Menotti: *Amahl and the Night Visitors—March of the Kings*, Gr. 1, Vol. 2

Amahl and the Night Visitors—Shepherd's Dance, Gr. 4, Vol. 2

Meyerbeer: *Les Patineurs—Waltz*, Gr. 2, Vol. 1

Milhaud: *Saudades do Brazil—Copacabana*, Gr. 4, Vol. 2

Saudades do Brazil—Laranjeiras, Gr. 2, Vol. 1

Suite Provençale—Modere (3rd movement), Gr. 1, Vol. 2

Moore: *Farm Journal—Harvest Song*, Gr. 1, Vol. 2

Moussorgsky: *Pictures at an Exhibition* (orchestrated by Ravel)—*Ballet of the Unhatched Chicks*, Gr. 1, Vol. 1; *Bydlo*, Gr. 2, Vol. 1; *Promenade No. 1*, Gr. 1, Vol. 2

Mozart: *Divertimento No. 17—Menuetto No. 1*, Gr. 5, Vol. 2

Eine kleine Nachtmusik—Romanze, Gr. 4, Vol. 1

The Little Nothings—Pantomime, Gr. 1, Vol. 2

Offenbach: *The Tales of Hoffman—Barcarolle*, Gr. 3, Vol. 1

Pierné: *Cydalise—Entrance of Little Fauns*, Gr. 2, Vol. 2

Prokofiev: *Children's Suite—Waltz on the Ice*, Gr. 3, Vol. 2

Summer Day Suite—March, Gr. 1, Vol. 1

Lieutenant Kije—Troika, Gr. 2, Vol. 2

Winter Holiday—Departure, Gr. 2, Vol. 1

Ravel: *Mother Goose Suite—The Conversations of Beauty and the Beast*, Gr. 5, Vol. 1

Mother Goose Suite—Laideronnette, Empress of the Pagodas, Gr. 4, Vol. 2

Respighi: *Brazilian Impressions—Danza*, Gr. 5, Vol. 2

Pines of Rome—Pines of the Villa Borghese, Gr. 4, Vol. 1

The Birds—Prelude, Gr. 2, Vol. 2

Rimsky-Korsakov: *Le Coq d'Or Suite—Bridal Procession,* Gr. 4, Vol. 1

Snow Maiden—Dance of the Buffoons, Gr. 2, Vol. 2

Rossini: *William Tell Overture—Finale,* Gr. 3, Vol. 1

Rossini-Britten: *Matinees Musicales—Waltz,* Gr. 1, Vol. 2

Soirées Musicales—Bolero, Gr. 2, Vol. 2

Soirées Musicales—March, Gr. 1, Vol. 1

Rossini-Respighi: *The Fantastic Toyshop—Can-Can,* Gr. 2, Vol. 1

The Fantastic Toyshop—Tarantella, Gr. 3, Vol. 2

Saint-Saëns: *Carnival of the Animals—The Elephant,* Gr. 1, Vol. 2

Carnival of the Animals—The Swan, Gr. 3, Vol. 2

Scarlatti-Tommasini: *The Good-Humored Ladies— Non Presto in Tempo di Ballo,* Gr. 4, Vol. 2

Schubert: *Symphony No. 5—First Movement,* Gr. 6, Vol. 1

Schuller: *Seven Studies on Themes of Paul Klee— Twittering Machine,* Gr. 2, Vol. 2

Schumann: *Scenes from Childhood—Träumerei,* Gr. 4, Vol. 2

Shostakovich: *Ballet Suite No. 1—Petite Ballerina,* Gr. 2, Vol. 1

Ballet Suite No. 1—Pizzicato Polka, Gr. 1, Vol. 1

Sibelius: *Karelia Suite—Alla Marcia,* Gr. 5, Vol. 1

Smetana: *The Bartered Bride—Dance of the Comedians,* Gr. 6, Vol. 2

Sousa: *Semper Fidelis,* Gr. 3, Vol. 2

The Stars and Stripes Forever, Gr. 4, Vol. 2

Strauss, R.: *Der Rosenkavalier—Suite,* Gr. 6, Vol. 1

Stravinsky: *The Firebird Suite—Berceuse,* Gr. 1, Vol. 1

The Firebird Suite—Infernal Dance of King Kastchei, Gr. 5, Vol. 2

Petrouchka—Russian Dance, Gr. 1, Vol. 2

Taylor: *Through the Looking Glass—Garden of Live Flowers,* Gr. 3, Vol. 2

Tchaikovsky: *Nutcracker Suite—Dance of the Sugar Plum Fairy,* Gr. 1, Vol. 2

Nutcracker Suite—Dance of the Reed Flutes, Gr. 1, Vol. 2

The Sleeping Beauty—Puss-in-Boots, The White Cat, Gr. 3, Vol. 1

The Sleeping Beauty—Waltz, Gr. 4, Vol. 1

Swan Lake—Dance of the Little Swans, Gr. 1, Vol. 1

Symphony No. 4—Fourth Movement, Gr. 6, Vol. 2

Thomson: *Acadian Songs and Dances—The Alligator and the 'Coon,* Gr. 3, Vol. 2

Acadian Songs and Dances—Walking Song, Gr. 1, Vol. 1

Vaughan Williams: *Fantasia on "Greensleeves,"* Gr. 6, Vol. 2

The Wasps—March Past of the Kitchen Utensils, Gr. 3, Vol. 1

Villa-Lobos: *Bachianas Brasileiras No. 2—The Little Train of Caipira,* Gr. 3, Vol. 1

Wagner: *Lohengrin—Prelude to Act III,* Gr. 6, Vol. 1

Walton: *Façade Suite—Valse,* Gr. 6, Vol. 2

Webern: *Five Movements for String Orchestra—Sehr Langsam* (4th movement), Gr. 2, Vol. 2

Bowmar Orchestral Library Contents

Alford: *Colonel Bogey March,* BOL #54

Bach: *Chorale, Awake, Thou Wintry Earth,* BOL #83

Jesu, Joy of Man's Desiring, BOL #62

Little Fugue in G Minor, BOL #86

Bartók: *Three Compositions,* BOL #68

Beethoven: *Symphony No. 5, First Movement,* BOL #72

Symphony No. 7, Scherzo, BOL #62

Symphony No. 8, Second Movement, BOL #71

Benjamin: *Jamaican Rumba,* BOL #56

Berlioz: *Hungarian March, Rakoczy,* BOL #54

March to the Scaffold, Symphonie Fantastique, BOL #78

Roman Carnival Overture, BOL #76

Bernstein: *Danzon, Fancy Free,* BOL #74

Symphonic Dances, excerpts, West Side Story, BOL #74

Bizet: *Carillon, L'Arlesienne Suite No. 1,* BOL #78

Farandole, L'Arlesienne Suite No. 2, BOL #78

Impromptu—The Top, Jeaux d'Enfants, BOL #53

March—Trumpet and Drum, Jeaux d'Enfants, BOL #53

Minuet, L'Arlesienne Suite No. 1, BOL #78

Prelude to Act I, Carmen, BOL #78

Borodin: *Excerpts, Polovetsian Dances, Prince Igor*, BOL #78

On the Steppes of Central Asia, BOL #78

Brahms: *Academic Festival Overture*, BOL #76

Hungarian Dance No. 5, BOL #55

Hungarian Dance No. 6, BOL #62

Piano Concerto No. 2, Fourth Movement, BOL #84

Symphony No. 3, Third Movement, BOL #71

Britten: *A Simple Symphony, First Movement*, BOL #72

Young Person's Guide to the Orchestra, BOL #83

Cailliet: *Pop! Goes the Weasel*, BOL #65

Castelnuovo-Tedesco: *Guitar Concerto, Second Movement*, BOL #84

Coates: *Cinderella*, BOL #57

London Suite—Covent Garden, Westminster, Knightsbridge March, BOL #60

Three Bears, BOL #67

Copland: *Hoe-Down, Rodeo*, BOL #55

A Lincoln Portrait, BOL #75

El Salon Mexico, BOL #74

Shaker Tune, Appalachian Spring, BOL #65

Corelli: *Badinerie*, BOL #56

Corelli-Pinelli: *Suite for String Orchestra, Sarabande, Gigue, Badinerie*, BOL #63

Couperin: *Little Windmills*, BOL #64

Debussy: *Children's Corner Suite*, BOL #63

Clair de Lune, BOL #52

Clouds, BOL #70

Dialogue of the Wind and the Sea, La Mer, BOL #70

En Bateau ("In a Boat"), BOL #53

Festivals, BOL #70

Donaldson: *Ballet Petit*, BOL #53

The Emperor's Nightingale, BOL #66

Harbor Vignettes, Fog and Storm, Song of the Bell Buoy, Sailing, BOL #53

Moon Legend, BOL #67

Once upon a Time Suite, Chicken Little, Three Billy Goats Gruff, Little Train, Hare and the Tortoise, BOL #52

Season Fantasies, Magic Piper, The Poet and His Lyre, The Anxious Leaf, The Snowmaiden, BOL #52

Under the Big Top, Marching Band, Acrobats, Juggler, Merry-Go-Round, Elephants, Clowns, Camels, Tightrope Walker, Pony Trot, Marching Band, BOL #51

Dukas: *Sorcerer's Apprentice*, BOL #59

Dvořák: *Slavonic Dance No. 1*, BOL #59

Symphony No. 9, From the New World, First Movement, BOL #72

Elgar: *Pomp and Circumstance, No. 1*, BOL #54

Elwell: *Dance of the Merry Dwarfs, Happy Hypocrite*, BOL #64

Folk Tune: *Sakura*, BOL #66

Gabrieli: *Canzona in C Major for Brass Ensemble and Organ*, BOL #83

Gershwin: *An American in Paris*, BOL #74

Gliere: *Russian Sailor's Dance, The Red Poppy*, BOL #78

Gould: *American Salute*, BOL #65

Gounod: *Funeral March of the Marionettes*, BOL #64

Grainger: *Londonderry Air*, BOL #60

Grieg: *Little Bird*, BOL #52

March of the Dwarfs, BOL #52

Norwegian Dance in A, No. 2, BOL #63

Peer Gynt Suite No. 1, Morning, Ase's Death, Anitra's Dance, In the Hall of the Mountain King, BOL #59

Piano Concerto, First Movement, BOL #84

Wedding Day at Troldhaugen, BOL #62

Grofé: *Grand Canyon Suite, Sunrise, Painted Desert, On the Trail, Sunset, Cloudburst*, BOL #61

Mississippi Suite, Father of the Waters, Huckleberry Finn, Old Creole Days, Mardi Gras, BOL #61

Guarnieri: *Dança Brasiliera*, BOL #55

Guion: *Arkansas Traveler*, BOL #56

Handel: *Bourrée, Fireworks Music*, BOL #62

A Ground, BOL #53

Hanson: *Symphony No. 2, Romantic, Second Movement*, BOL #72

Harris: *Folk Song Symphony, Interlude*, BOL #75

Haydn: *Gypsy Rondo*, BOL #64

Symphony No. 99, BOL #73

"Surprise" Symphony, Variations, BOL #62

"Surprise" Symphony, Minuet, BOL #63

Holst: *Mercury, The Planets*, BOL #70

Humperdinck: *Hansel and Gretel Overture*, BOL #58

Ippolitov-Ivanov: *Cortege of the Sardar, Caucasian Sketches*, BOL #54

In the Village, Caucasian Sketches, BOL #78

Ives: *Symphony No. 2, Last Movement*, BOL #65
 Putnam's Camp, Three Places in New England, BOL #75

Kabalevsky: *Gavotte*, BOL #55
 Intermezzo, The Comedians, BOL #53

Khatchaturian: *Galop, Masquerade Suite*, BOL #55
 Mazurka, Masquerade Suite, BOL #55
 Russian Dance, Gayne Suite No. 2, BOL #56

Kodály: *Háry János Suite, Viennese Musical Clock, Battle and Defeat of Napoleon, Intermezzo, Entrance of the Emperor*, BOL #81

Koyama: *Woodcutter's Song*, BOL #66

Kraft: *Theme and Variation for Percussion Quartet*, BOL #83

Lecocq: *Can-Can Grand Waltz, Mlle. Angot Suite*, BOL #56
 Gavotte, Mlle. Angot Suite, BOL #53
 Polka, Mlle. Angot Suite, BOL #53

Leo: *Arietta*, BOL #64

Liadov: *Dance of the Mosquito*, BOL #52
 Music Box, BOL #64
 Village Dance, BOL #53

McBride: *Pumpkin-Eater's Little Fugue*, BOL #65

Mahler: *Symphony No. 1, Second Movement*, BOL #62

Mendelssohn: *Violin Concerto, Third Movement*, BOL #84
 Scherzo, Midsummer Night's Dream, BOL #57

Menotti: *Suite from Amahl and the Night Visitors, Introduction, March of the Three Kings, Dance of the Shepherds*, BOL #58

Moussorgsky: *Night on Bald Mountain*, BOL #82
 Pictures at an Exhibition, BOL #82

Mozart: *Minuet*, BOL #53
 Overture, The Marriage of Figaro, BOL #76
 Romanze, A Little Night Music, BOL #86
 Symphony No. 40, First Movement, BOL #71
 Symphony No. 40, Minuet, BOL #62
 Theme and Variations, Serenade for Wind Instruments, K361, BOL #83

Phillips: *Midnight Ride of Paul Revere, Selections from McGuffy's Readers*, BOL #75

Pierné: *Entrance of the Little Fauns*, BOL #54
 March of the Little Lead Soldiers, BOL #54

Pinto: *Memories of Childhood*, BOL #68

Prokofiev: *Cinderella, Sewing Scene, Cinderella's Gavotte, Midnight Waltz, Fairy Godmother*, BOL #67

Classical Symphony, BOL #73
 Lieutenant Kije, Birth of Kije, Troika, BOL #81
 March, BOL #54
 March, The Love for Three Oranges, BOL #54

Ravel: *Mother Goose Suite, Pavane of the Sleeping Beauty, Hop o' My Thumb, Laideronette, Empress of the Pagodas, Beauty and the Beast, The Fairy Garden*, BOL #57
 Suite No. 2, Daphnes and Chloe, BOL #86

Respighi: *The Birds, Prelude*, BOL #85
 Fountains of Rome, BOL #85
 Pines of Rome, BOL #85

Rimsky-Korsakov: *Flight of the Bumble Bee*, BOL #52
 Scheherezade, BOL #77

Rodgers: *The March of the Siamese Children, The King and I*, BOL #54

Rossini: *Overture, William Tell*, BOL #76

Rossini-Respighi: *Pizzicato, Fantastic Toyshop*, BOL #53
 Tarantella, Fantastic Toyshop, BOL #56
 Waltz, Fantastic Toyshop, BOL #56

Saint-Saens: *Carnival of the Animals, Introduction, Royal March of the Lion, Hens and Cocks, Fleet Footed Animals, Turtles, The Elephant, Kangaroos, Aquarium, Long Eared Personages, Cuckoo in the Deep Woods, Aviary, Pianists, Fossils, The Swan, Finale*, BOL #51
 Danse Macabre, BOL #59
 Symphony No. 3, Fourth Movement, BOL #71
 Phaeton, BOL #59

Schoenberg: *Peripetia, Five Pieces for Orchestra*, BOL #86

Schubert: *The Bee*, BOL #64
 Marche Militaire, BOL #54
 Symphony No. 5, Minuet, BOL #62
 "Trout" Quintet, Fourth Movement, BOL #83

Schuman: *Chester, New England Triptych*, BOL #75

Schumann: *The Happy Farmer*, BOL #64
 Symphony No. 4, Second Movement, BOL #71
 Träumerei, BOL #63
 The Wild Horseman, BOL #64

Schumann-Glazounov: *Chopin, Carnival*, BOL #53
 German Waltz-Paganini, Carnival, BOL #53

Sibelius: *Finlandia*, BOL #60
 Symphony No. 2, First Movement, BOL #72

Smetana: *Dance of the Comedians*, BOL #56
 The Moldau, BOL #60

Sousa: *The Stars and Stripes Forever*, BOL #54

Strauss: *Overture, The Bat*, BOL #76
    Tritsch-Tratsch Polka, BOL #56
    Till Eulenspiegel, BOL #81
Stravinsky: *Circus Polka*, BOL #1 (Animals and
    Circus)
    Devil Dance, BOL #68
    *Firebird Suite, Koschai's Enchanted Garden, Dance
    of the Firebird, Dance of the Princesses, Infernal
    Dance of King Koschai, Magic Sleep of the Princess Tzarevna, Finale (Escape of Koschai's Captive)*, BOL #69
    Palace of the Chinese Emperor, The Nightingale,
    BOL #69
    Petrouchka, complete ballet score with narrative,
    BOL #80
    Tango, The Soldier's Tale, BOL #69
    Village Festival, The Fairy's Kiss, BOL #69
    Waltz and Ragtime, The Soldier's Tale, BOL #69
Tchaikovsky: *Album for the Young*, BOL #68
    The Lark Song, Scenes of Youth, BOL #52
    *Nutcracker Suite, Overture Miniature, March,
    Dance of the Sugar Plum Fairy, Trepak, Arabian
    Dance, Chinese Dance, Dance of the Toy Flutes,
    Waltz of the Flowers*, BOL #58
    Romeo and Juliet, BOL #86
    Sleeping Beauty Waltz, BOL #67
    Symphony No. 4, Third Movement, BOL #71
Thomson: *Cattle and Blues, Plow That Broke the
    Plains*, BOL #65
    *Fugue and Chorale on Yankee Doodle, Tuesday

in November, BOL #65
    Seapiece with Birds, BOL #70
Torjussen: *Folk Song, Fjord and Mountain, Norwegian Suite No. 2*, BOL #60
    Lapland Idyll, BOL #60
    To the Rising Sun, Fjord and Mountain, Norwegian Suite No. 2, BOL #52
Vaughan Williams: *Folk Dances from Somerset,
    English Folk Song Suite*, BOL #56
Verdi: *Anvil Chorus*, BOL #63
Villa-Lobos: *Little Train of the Caipira*, BOL #64
Vivaldi: *Concerto in C for Two Trumpets, First Movement*, BOL #84
Wagner: *Overture, The Flying Dutchman*, BOL #70
    Lohengrin, Overture to Act 1, Prelude to Act 3,
    BOL #79
    Love Death, Tristan and Isolde, BOL #79
    *The Mastersingers of Nuremberg, Prelude, Dance
    of the Apprentices and Entrance of the Mastersingers*, BOL #79
    Ride of the Valkyries, BOL #62
    Siegfried's Rhine Journey, Twilight of the Gods,
    BOL #79
Waldteufel: *España Waltz*, BOL #56
    Skater's Waltz, BOL #55
Walton: *Façade Suite, Polka, Country Dance, Popular
    Song*, BOL #55
Wolf-Ferrari: *Dance of the Comedians*, BOL #55
Zador: *Children's Symphony*, BOL #64

Classified Song Index

SONGS FOR AUTOHARP

1 Chord

Are You Sleeping, 160, 233
Canoe Song, 123, 173, 178
Little Tom Tinker, 61
Scotland's Burning, 62, 159, 235
Shalom Chaverim, 63
Ten in the Bed, 235

2 Chords

Bluebird through My Window, 229
Bounce Around, 134, 138, 139
Cockles and Mussels, 246
The Cuckoo, 28, 107
Down by the Station, 30, 110
Down in the Valley, 65
Draw a Bucket of Water, 160, 231
Goodby, Old Paint, 116
Go Tell Aunt Rhody, 71, 159, 228
Go to Sleep, 21, 70, 106
Hot Cross Buns, 70, 153, 159, 220, 224
Little Shepherds, 64
London Bridge, 20, 138
Michael Finnegan, 237
My Hat, 241

On a Mountain Stands a Lady, 161, 232–233
Sweet Potato, 214

3 Chords

Adam Had Seven Sons, 236
All Night, All Day, 244
All the Pretty Little Horses, 114
Bingo, 86
Blackeyed Susie, 66
Bought Me a Dog, 41, 200
Ezekiel Saw a Wheel, 47
Fire Down Below, 39
Get on Board, 242
Grandpa's Whiskers, 240
Hey Betty Martin, 161, 227
Hill and Gully Rider, 101
Hop Up! My Ladies, 27, 109
If You're Happy, 231
I'm Gonna Sing, 46
I Saw Three Ships, 245
John Henry, 100
The Keeper, 28–29
Mama Don't 'Low, 200, 217
Mary Had a Baby, 238
Michael, Row, 35
Music Alone Shall Live, 36
New River Train, 25

SONGS AND MELODIES FOR MELODY INSTRUMENTS

Sol–Fa and Rhythm Syllable Guide

The following guide serves as a reference for students and teachers who use a vocal approach to music literacy. The guide includes specific melodic and rhythmic patterns written in sol–fa or rhythm syllables (see Chapter 12). Below each pattern is a list of songs that contain clear examples of each pattern. Numbers inside the parentheses indicate the measures in which the patterns appear.

MELODIC PATTERNS

s-m

Bluebird through My Window (1,5), 229
Bought Me a Dog (7), 41, 200
Lemonade, 224
New River Train (1), 25
Rain, Rain Go Away, 224

s-m-s

John Kanaka (17,19), 160, 224
This Old Man (1), 162

m-s

Johnny, Are You Ready? (1), 236
Turn Your Glasses Over (9), 200, 211

s-l-s

The Whistle of the Train (1), 38

s-l-s-m

Bluebird through My Window (2,4,6), 229
Hill and Gully Rider (1,3), 101
On a Mountain Stands a Lady (1,2,5,6), 161, 232–233

d-m-s

Bought Me a Dog (1), 41, 200
Kum Bah Yah (2,4), 237

d-s

Down by the Station (13), 30, 110

♪♩ ♪

♫♩.

♬ (3)

♬♬

♫♫

♬♫

♩.♫

♩.

6/8

9/8

3/4

3/4 + 2/4

Alphabetical Song Index

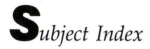

Subject Index